30 DAYS
CHALLENGE

*Step by Step: Women's 30 Day
Guide to Success*

curated by
STACEY HALL

with

ADRIENNE HILL | ANTJE SWART | BRENDA
MARTINO | CHERI PETRONI | DARLENE WILLIAMS
| DONNA BARRON | DORTHA HISE
| DR. CAROLINA M. BILLINGS | DR. PATRICIA
SUGGS | KIM RILEY | LORALEE HUMPHREYS | M.
SUSAN PATTERSON | MONIKA GRECZEK | RAJIKA
MAHAN | STACEY HALL | STEPHANIE ODEN

produced by
DR. CAROLINA M. BILLINGS

30 Days Challenge by Powerful Women Today

Published by PWT Publishing

A division of Powerful Women Today

3 Centre St. #202, Markham, ON

L3P 3P9 Canada

Publisher: Dr. Carolina M. Billings'
email: publisher@powerfulwomentoday.com

Limits of Liability and Disclaimer of Warranty

Disclaimer

ISBN:

Paperback ISBN: 978-1-7382310-4-1

eBook ISBN: 978-1-7382310-3-4

CONTENTS

"Think like a queen. A queen is not afraid to fail. Failure is another stepping stone to greatness."
— **Oprah Winfrey**

PREFACE

By Judy Cirullo

"Nothing is impossible. The word itself says 'I'm possible!"

Audrey Hepburn's quote, "Nothing is impossible. The word itself says 'I'm possible!'" encapsulates the essence of resilience and optimism crucial for success. It's a reminder that challenges are surmountable, and by altering one's perspective, the seemingly unattainable becomes achievable. Embracing a mindset where possibilities outweigh obstacles paves the way for triumph.

As you embrace the challenges in this book, you might ask yourself, "What do I NEED to do vs. what do I WANT to do to become more resilient, optimistic, and forward-thinking while embracing the obstacles that might appear insurmountable?"

As the landscape continues to fluctuate in 2024, setting yourself up for success can be challenging. But as you begin to craft your plan, you must first define a delicate balance between your personal and professional growth. While a list of things might be nice and easy for me to share without first defining what you WANT or NEED, the list can become just another list.

Why is identifying your WANT vs. your NEED essential, and should be your first step on your plan? Because we often associate success with happiness, and happiness is something you think you NEED to go out and get. Research shows that happiness is where you start, not where you finish. This means that when we constantly tell ourselves that we NEED to get to this or accomplish that to be successful, it creates an unhealthy attachment to something external. This creates more stress, and you are pulled away from acknowledging the value of what you have already accomplished in the past. The reality is the true measurement of your progress is what you have done in the past.

By shifting your mindset and embracing a WANT to approach to your future, resources, creativity, and innovation open up. You become empowered and gain control over what you WANT. When you approach your goals from a WANT to, your passion and purpose drive your motivation. Thus, your WANT to is internal to you; you control the journey with the end in mind.

Now it is time to explore an exercise that you can do to create your success criteria and filter it down based on WANT to vs. NEED to. As you prepare to complete this one-page exercise, Start with this statement: "I'm being successful when"... Then, click the link to download the worksheet that guides you in defining your success criteria.

Judy Cirullo, PT, ACC, CPC, C-IQ
Certified Seasoned Executive & Team Culture Coach at Grow Strong Teams

Connect with Judy on LinkedIn:
https://www.linkedin.com/in/judycirullo/

According to the Greek myth,
Sisyphus
is condemned to roll a rock
up to the top of a mountain,
only to have the rock
roll back down
to the bottom
every time
he reaches the top.
The gods were wise,
in perceiving
that an eternity
of futile labour
repeating
the same
task,
the same way
is a hideous
punishment.

Le mythe de Sisyphe
By Albert Camus

"It took me quite a long time to develop a voice, and now that I have it, I am not going to be silent."
— **Madeleine Albright**

INTRODUCTION

A 30-day commitment is effective for habit formation because it establishes consistency, allows for brain adaptation, helps overcome initial resistance, integrates the habit into your routine, enhances psychological commitment, and enables you to see tangible results. By focusing on maintaining the habit for 30 days, you increase the likelihood of making it a permanent part of your lifestyle.

1. Establishing Consistency
Repetition: Consistently performing a behaviour for 30 days helps ingrain it into your daily routine. Repetition is key to habit formation as it creates a pattern that becomes easier to follow over time.

2. Building Neural Pathways
Brain Adaptation: The brain needs time to rewire itself to accommodate new behaviours. 30 days is typically sufficient for the brain to start forming new neural pathways, making the new habit feel more natural and automatic.

3. Overcoming Initial Resistance
Breaking Through: The first few days of starting a new habit are often the hardest due to resistance and discomfort. By committing to 30 days, you give yourself enough time to push through these initial barriers and make the new behavior less daunting.

4. Creating a Routine
Integration: A 30-day period allows the new habit to be integrated into your daily life. This timeframe is long enough to test the habit in various contexts and conditions, ensuring it can be sustained.

5. Psychological Commitment
Mental Endurance: Committing to 30 days can enhance your psychological commitment. It's a manageable timeframe that isn't too overwhelming, yet long enough to see significant progress and results, boosting motivation.

6. Seeing Results
Motivation: Within 30 days, you're likely to start seeing the benefits of your new habit. Whether it's improved fitness, better productivity, or enhanced well-being, these positive outcomes reinforce the habit and motivate continued adherence.

In the chapters that follow you will see a pathway to Success, Personal Development: Becoming your best-self, the link between Wellness and Mindset and finally how all of the above link and impact your relationships.

Antje Swart gets us started by guiding us on *How to Get More of What you Want.* This chapter is a guide offering a practical approach to harnessing the mind's power to take action toward any goal. Scientific evidence and personal success stories prove success is accessible to everyone. Addressing this universal quest for achievement, readers will discover how to focus their thoughts, emotions, and actions towards attaining goal-orientated milestones and a fulfilling life. By cultivating self-awareness and focusing on what we already possess, we can direct our internal states toward desired outcomes. The 30-Day Challenge encourages specific journaling to manifest desires through focused attention on our current blessings so we can manifest more.

Adrienne Hill inspires us to *Explode Your Business Audience & Income* Many online business owners struggle to build an audience that is big enough to fuel their income goals. Despite the recent rise in technology, they struggle to find high-quality leads and are not able to find their ideal clients. With much effort and nonstop "hustle," they often enter a phase of frustration and burnout, and many of them fail to keep their businesses alive. In this chapter, I'll break down the online strategy that is most effective in bringing in leads, building relationships, and generating consistent clients and cash flow.

Stephanie Oden helps us to *Elevate Your Self-Belief as an Introvert Entrepreneur*. This chapter empowers introverted entrepreneurs to embrace their introversion as a superpower, challenging societal conditioning and limiting beliefs that undermine self-confidence. By reflecting on personal experiences and presenting research, the chapter demonstrates that introversion is not a flaw but a strength. It offers actionable strategies to elevate self-belief. With the guidance in this chapter, readers will transform their self-perception, unlocking their full potential to achieve entrepreneurial success.

Dr. Patricia Suggs reminds us *How to Open the Glass Doors to More Promotions and Raises* Women 55+ who bring a wealth of knowledge and expertise but face unique challenges in the workplace, being pushed aside for promotions, and navigating conflicts that arise in diverse work environments. Effective conflict reconciliation skills enable them to maintain strong professional relationships, foster team collaboration, and handle disagreements constructively. These skills can support career advancement by showcasing leadership capabilities, emotional intelligence, and the ability to navigate complex situations with diplomacy and tact.

Overall, these skills empower professional women 55+ to open the glass doors, navigate challenges effectively, build successful working relationships, and contribute positively to the workplace.

Dr. Carolina M. Billings challenges us to *Become a LinkedIn Subject Matter Expert.* This chapter offers a comprehensive, step-by-step plan to transform your LinkedIn profile and establish yourself as a Subject Matter Expert and Thought Leader within a month. You'll learn how to optimize your profile, create compelling content, engage with your audience, and strategically grow your network. Becoming a thought leader on LinkedIn is vital because it significantly boosts your professional credibility, visibility, and influence. As the leading professional and business networking platform, LinkedIn is essential for showcasing your expertise, connecting with industry peers, and staying ahead of industry trends. Following this guide, you will elevate your brand's impact and unlock new opportunities within meaningful professional relationships.

Dortha Hise empowers us to find balance in our lives by *Reclaiming 4 Hours a Week.* This chapter guides high-achieving entrepreneurial and executive women in reclaiming 4 hours a week through effective delegation and intentional scheduling. Utilizing techniques in shifting mindsets, embracing trust in their teams, and practical delegation techniques, readers will discover how to free up significant time. The 30-day challenge encourages strategic task management, allowing focus on high-impact activities and personal well-being. With these changes, readers will experience improved productivity, deeper personal connections, enhanced mental wellness, and a stronger, more autonomous team, ultimately leading to more balance and fulfillment in all areas of their lives.

Rajika Mahan begins the journey of self-transformation with *The Power of Your Self-Image*. This chapter focuses on the transformative journey of shifting a previously-held perception of oneself that is no longer serving its purpose. It highlights the importance of assisting and supporting women in choosing to present themselves with elevated self-esteem, confidence and clarity. By doing so, they are empowered to break free from self-imposed constraints, beliefs, and patterns so that they can step out from behind these limiting factors.

Brenda Martino concludes the first half of our compilation with her inspiring words on *How to Elevate by Finding the Missing Pieces of Yourself* Within this chapter you will find techniques to help you prepare for whatever life has in store for you by ensuring you have discovered your missing pieces. "I know what it's like to be unprepared. In my late 40s, I began to feel discontented with life. I started a journey to discover what was going on within me. Then, my husband was diagnosed and died from cancer. Not only was I grieving but I felt unprepared for life. I kept searching and trying different things until I finally discovered my missing piece so now, I can help you find yours."

So, let's begin...

"I am no longer accepting the things I cannot change. I am changing the things I cannot accept."
— Angela Davis

Part 1: Success

ANTJE SWART

Dedication
To my children who always remind me what is really
important in life

CHAPTER 1

HOW TO HAVE MORE OF WHAT YOU WANT

By Antje Swart

Why do some individuals achieve their goals while others stumble at every turn?

This question takes us to the basic principles of success. Is it an innate talent or something more accessible for everyone? Maslow's hierarchy of needs indicates mankind has a universal quest for happiness and fulfillment. The definition of fulfillment, joy, and wealth vary from person to person, yet the desire for success is universal.

This quest for success begins in the mind, which together with the body, is like a super machine. We have thoughts and the body is the physical expression of our habitual thinking patterns.

The mind operates on two levels: the subconscious, which regulates automatic processes and holds deep-seated beliefs, and the conscious, which provides logic and serves as a gatekeeper, filtering information based on learned experiences. The subconscious absorbs experiences in childhood as programming that shape our beliefs and habits. These are not fixed and can be updated or changed.

We are not merely products of our thoughts and emotions but the architects of them. By cultivating self-awareness, we can direct our thoughts, emotions, and actions towards desired outcomes. Success, therefore, is not a matter of inherent talent, but of conscious focus and alignment of our internal states with our actions, leading to tangible achievements. Such focus best starts by paying attention to what you already have, because you have been successful in acquiring it. The object of your desire is already in your possession, which serves as proof of success.

Like it or not. Money is a symbol of Success

Aligning our thoughts, emotions, and actions towards achieving financial success is crucial because it directly impacts our ability to live a fulfilling life, as highlighted by Robert Byrne's saying, "The purpose of life is a life of purpose".

Financial resources play a significant role in moving us from merely surviving to thriving and achieving self-actualization. Money, a symbol of success, facilitates a richer life experience by enabling access to essentials and luxuries alike. However, the desire for financial abundance is often in conflict with underlying emotional fears, creating a cycle of gain and loss. While a person consciously wants more riches in their life, often there are negatively charged underlying beliefs around being truly wealthy.

This conflict can leave individuals feeling powerless, resigned to mediocrity, or worse, trapped in poverty. The key to breaking this cycle lies in mastering the power of focus, to align our desires with our thoughts and actions. This alignment is not limited by age, gender, or nationality, making it a universally applicable solution.

Understanding and harnessing this power can lead to a life of growth, contribution, and connection, embodying our deepest desires. It enables us to realize our potential, make a positive impact, and live in accordance with our values and aspirations. Therefore, aligning our thoughts, emotions, and actions is not just about achieving financial success; it's about unlocking the door to a meaningful and purpose-driven life.

The ability to change our brains.

Hebb's Rule states: when a cell persistently activates another nearby cell, the connection between the two cells becomes stronger. This process is fundamental in changing your brain chemistry through consistent focus on specific thoughts.

Albert Einstein discovered that all matter is energy at the most fundamental levels, which means that you can influence matter through thought energy.

Dr. Joe Despenza's ongoing research clearly demonstrates the impact meditation (focused thought and emotion) can have on immunity (August 2023, Vienna, Dr Hemal), showing how thoughts and emotions are influencing cell structure.

At Princeton University, Robert Jahn and Brenda Dunne conducted rigorous experiments for over a decade, demonstrating that human consciousness can influence physical reality. Their research demonstrated mental concentration could affect the operation of machines, providing empirical evidence for the interaction between mind and matter.

Add to this equation Carl Jung's findings that a person's life is the history of the self-expression of the unconscious, and that everything in the unconscious is expressed by incidents in the person's life or external phenomena. Everything we dream about can happen, to the extent that the unconscious interprets the energy of the universe.

The placebo effect serves as a scientific parallel, demonstrating how the brain's response to belief can manifest physical outcomes, mirroring the process of achieving success through focused thought, emotion, and action.

There is overwhelming evidence that our focused thoughts and emotions can in fact alter matter as they become stronger with repetition and practice over time.

Sharing my personal journey.

These scientific studies and many others prove success is a direct result of specific mental focus, emotional states and aligned action.

Napoleon Hill's book "Think and Grow Rich" has been a global best-seller for more than 100 years and showcases the power of aligning head, heart, and habits to focus on a specific outcome, which has helped millions of people to change their lives for the better.

My personal journey from South Africa to Sweden shows the practical application of these principles. By focusing my thoughts, supporting them with positive emotions, and taking strategic actions, I was able to secure a furnished house within my budget and in the perfect location, all before physically moving to Sweden. I was moving to a student town with a family of 4 and after arrival we learned that it apparently is very difficult to secure housing on short notice. It only took me about 5 weeks. This process was not reliant on luck, but a deliberate application of focused thought (head), joyful expectation (heart), and strategic action (habit).

The subsequent smooth acquisition of a house that met all my specified criteria further underscores the power of this approach. This calculated use of thoughts, emotions, and actions to manifest desired outcomes demonstrates the tangible results that can be achieved when one aligns their head, heart, and habit in pursuit of their goals.

During my service as coach and therapist I have furthermore witnessed many people meeting their dream partner, advancing a career, creating great relationships as a result of practicing the technique I'm sharing here with you as a 30-Day Challenge.

Your 30-Day Challenge

During this 30-day Challenge, you will discover how to use the power of your subconscious and analytical mind through deliberate focus.

This practice involves leveraging the energetic power of thoughts and emotions to manifest desired outcomes. The nature of transferring thought energy into matter means that focusing on what you already have amplifies your ability to attract more of the same.

To reinforce this process, journal your thoughts and feelings of having. Having means to focus on what you already successfully acquired (have) and the positive emotions these possessions evoke, thus transforming you into a powerful magnet for attraction.

Writing this down gives it a physical form, setting the stage for manifestation. Manifestation implies making something evident or visible. By documenting what you have and how it makes you feel, you initiate the first step towards bringing more of the same into reality. You are also finding proof that you can manifest.

Start your journal entries with statements like "I have [---], and it makes me feel [---]." This practice gradually charges your electromagnetic field, turning you into an attraction powerhouse.

As you grow more conscious of your current blessings and the joy they bring you, it becomes easier to attract more of them into your world.

Do this simple yet profound technique for 30 days, 10 min per day or more and witness the shift in your energy, mindset and the results you are achieving.

For more detailed tips about supercharging your journaling click here: https://watchmesucceed.online/journaling-tips

About the Author

Antje Swart is supporting people to experience more fulfillment, joy and wealth. As the creator of the "WATCH ME Succeed" process and a licensed therapist, Antje's journey is dedicated to helping others overcome a myriad of challenges, including fears, stress, burnout, and depression. Her approach is comprehensive, offering personalized sessions, group coaching, online courses, and audio tracks to ensure ongoing support.

Antje's expertise is vast and through her personal experiences as a mother, wife, and business professional, she has made hundreds of transformations possible while crafting fulfilling lives.

The loss of her partner in 2021 was a turning point for Antje as she navigated through this profound personal crisis. This time of darkness led her to apply her accumulated knowledge and skills to rebuild her life and that of her children. Through this process, she identified 7 strategic steps essential for creating a new, fulfilling existence.

Her mission is to unlock the potential within each individual, aiding them in navigating their unique paths to success and well-being. Antje Swart's story is not just one of overcoming adversity, but also of using her experiences to light the way for others on their journey to personal and professional growth.

Antje Swart
Consciousness Elevator
antjeswart@consciousnesselevator.com
https://www.linkedin.com/in/antje-swart/

ADRIENNE HILL

Dedication
This chapter is dedicated to my husband, Rob. He is my #1
supporter in life.

CHAPTER 2

EXPLODE YOUR BUSINESS AUDIENCE & INCOME

By Adrienne Hill

As business ownership evolves, technology is moving faster than ever and online tools, strategies, and systems are changing rapidly. A thriving business is (and always will be) based on relationship building. But the way we build relationships is night and day different than it was even 20 short years ago.

In the 1900s and early 2000s, relationship building in business largely revolved around attending networking groups and in-person events. The 2010s era brought us social media and online relationship building. The covid pandemic forced big and small businesses alike to embrace remote working & connection solutions (such as zoom) and forced many businesses to pivot into the online space if they had not already. And now in the 2020s with the introduction of A.I. and high-tech CRMs, it's become about collecting leads on a mass scale and sorting through thousands of them to find interested people, and then to relationship build and network with only the most qualified leads.

And yet, with all of these changes that should make business building easier, more people than ever are struggling. The #1 complaint most business owners have is that they "can't find enough of the right people who want my offers or services". In a world where we can literally connect with thousands of people in a moment's notice, how can this be possible?!

Making real authentic connections

In the simplest sense, people are craving real, authentic connection more than ever. Yet at the same time, their attention spans are so short, they are unable to focus long enough to get the connection they desperately need. Everyone is focused on being seen, heard, and understood....but nobody is taking the time to listen.

People are seeking instant gratification and want immediate results. As you can imagine, this both makes genuine moments of connection more difficult to create and also makes the task of sorting through leads to create genuine connection challenging.

Relationships are built one-on-one but technology is moving us in a direction of seeking quantity over quality. The tension this creates for business owners is unmistakable, especially for those who value quality over quantity or who do not consider themselves to be "techy".

On the flip side, business owners who value time freedom are seeking that balance between quantity and quality by embracing these leverage building tools. They are tired of the nonstop hustle and appreciate the freedom that comes with tech tools that help them to sort through the masses to find the highest quality connections.

Regardless of which side of the coin you fall on, those who

don't keep up will be left behind.

Did you know that 93% of communication is non-verbal?

Entrepreneur Magazine's take on relationship building in 2024 is that "digital networking will be essential, and your best qualities must be transmuted on video". This isn't very surprising when you consider that up to 93% of communication is actually nonverbal. Add in the digital world we live in, and video marketing is a no-brainer. Because of this, every business big and small is flocking to social media with the deep seated belief that simply showing up consistently is going to bring in revenue. Yet the common consensus is that simply showing up isn't enough. Learning the art of effective marketing is much harder than it appears on the surface.

Going deeper, they point out that social media, although powerful, is quickly becoming a "pay to play" resource given that "the algorithms do not allow average businesses to get in front of their desired avatar unless they invest money". So now, business owners are faced with learning the tougher-than-it-seems art of marketing AND they have to invest in paid exposure for it to reach enough people to matter.

And of top of that, most people on social media are simply there to be entertained, to get external validation by getting engagement on their content, or to simply pass the time in between other activities. They are typically NOT there to actively search for businesses and brands that offer solutions to their problems. Add up all of the above, and it's no wonder businesses are struggling!

Source:https://www.entrepreneur.com/growing-a-business/how-to-network-like-a-pro-in-2024/466834

Source:https://www.psychologytoday.com/us/blog/
beyond-words/201109/is-nonverbal-communication-a-
numbers-game

The Audience Explosion Launch & Scale System is the perfect solution for the tension between quality and quantity, while building moments of connection and powerful relationships. It brings in 1,000+ high quality, problem aware leads for businesses in only 2 weeks. It then sorts through them rapidly to find the people who are ready to pursue a solution, builds powerful moments of relationship and connection with the audience, and drives them towards booking calls or submitting applications to get their problems solved. And the best part is that this strategy works even if you are starting from scratch and have 0 followers, 0 email list, and 0 revenue when you start!

The basic premise of this strategy is to host a virtual summit or conference with a panel of expert speakers, to bring massive value to your online audience.

The basic premise of this strategy is to host a virtual summit or conference with a panel of expert speakers, to bring massive value to your online audience.

Shannon Lavenia, creator of the P.A.I.D. framework and Brand Builder A.I. activated this strategy and in less than a month brought in 1,647 leads, generated $12,559 in immediate cash flow, and signed another $35,000 worth of contracted clients via payment plans. Because of the relationship building aspect, she also created a new & powerful business partnership with the potential of bringing in 6-figures in business within the first year.

I myself have activated this launch strategy multiple times, and have brought in anywhere from $17,000 to $96,000 in a single month each time! I've also been able to build my marketing email list from 0 to over 16,000 people in only 3 years time!

Here's how to get started in the next 30 days:

1. **Days 1-10:** Identify a high value offer you would like to sell to your audience. The types of offers that work best are related to coaching, consulting, or done-for-you services. Then, get clear on the results people will get if they purchase your offer. This is not the best strategy for driving low cost product sales (better to go to Etsy or TikTok shop for those). If you are geographically limited in business, this won't be the best fit for you either.

2. **Days 11-20:** Make a list of up to 50 potential speakers in your industry or niche who are likely to have big followings and email lists. Don't pre-judge or assume they wouldn't want to speak at your event. Just brainstorm and give yourself permission to dream. The key is to find speakers who serve the same audience you do but in a different way, so that they are joining with a collaborative energy and not a competitive one.

3. **Days 21-30:** Sign up for the Audience Explosion Masterclass to learn the ins and outs of how this strategy works. After class, sign up for a free consultation with my team to assess if this strategy would be a good fit for you. As you can see from step #1 above, it's not a great fit for everyone, so we offer free consultations to help make sure it's a match. As a part of the assessment you'll

get an additional free training series to watch so you can hit the ground running!

The Audience Explosion Masterclass shows you how to:

1. Explode your Audience by 1,000+ organic, super HOT, and ready to buy leads in only 2 weeks...without ANY paid ads or "hustling" on social media!

2. Book Up with Calls or Applications with 5% of your new audience automatically signing up! Buckle your seatbelt!

3. Delegate & Scale 90% of the traffic generation activities to your support team to unlock more lifestyle freedom!

Get the masterclass here:
https://www.audience-explosion.com

About the Author

Adrienne built a career in corporate America managing multi-million dollar launches for Fortune 500 companies. She channeled that experience into creating and building out a structured, systematized approach to building her own brand online.

Using her proprietary system, she created an instant audience in the thousands and launched multiple programs which ALL scaled to 6-figure businesses in only 6 months each! She now focuses on helping entrepreneurs to build the skills, structure, and systems they need to build multi-million-dollar businesses and brands.

Adrienne is passionate about helping coaches, consultants, and service providers to make the smartest use of their limited time while they build their income to the point where they can live the dream life they've always wanted from their business.

When she's not working on her business you can find her hiking, fishing, traveling, or having outdoor adventures with her husband, adult children, and golden retriever puppies.

Adrienne Hill
Skills-Structure-Systems
support@skills-structure-systems.com

https://www.linkedin.com/company/skills-structure-systems/

STEPHANIE Y. ODEN

Dedication
To the quiet achievers who are changing the world.

CHAPTER 3:

ELEVATE YOUR SELF-BELIEF AS AN INTROVERT ENTREPRENEUR

By Stephanie Y. Oden

Returning to my childhood home, I spent time in my room, a place of solitude. As I reflected, memories of my youth and young adulthood resurfaced—times when I felt out of place, drained by social interactions, and burdened by the belief that something was inherently wrong with me.

This feeling of not fitting in, left me ashamed of my personality and consumed by loneliness and low self-confidence.

Even as a successful corporate leader, I faced constant suggestions to be more 'outgoing' and 'extroverted.' While I honed my leadership skills, these experiences reinforced the idea that my introversion was a flaw.

When I embarked on my entrepreneurial journey, my self-belief was a fragile mix of high achievement and presumed limitations.

However, introversion is not a flaw but a strength. Research shows that more people prefer introversion than extroversion, yet societal conditioning often undervalues introverted traits.

This conditioning leads many introvert entrepreneurs to internalize limiting beliefs, particularly around self-belief. These mental blocks, often rooted in past experiences and societal expectations, prevent them from reaching their full potential.

This chapter addresses the critical issue of low self-belief among introvert entrepreneurs. It offers practical strategies for recognizing, challenging, and reframing limiting beliefs. Empowering introverts to embrace their authentic selves, celebrate their unique strengths, and achieve entrepreneurial success.

In essence, transforming the way introvert entrepreneurs view themselves. By elevating self-belief, it unlocks the true potential of introvert entrepreneurs, enabling them to navigate their entrepreneurial journey with confidence and achieve their dreams.

Breaking through with awareness at the forefront.

As I transitioned into entrepreneurship, these ingrained beliefs held me back. I believed my introversion was a limitation, a flaw that needed fixing.

This mindset was reinforced by the societal preference for extroverted traits, making me doubt my potential. However, the crucial truth: introversion is not a flaw but a strength.

According to data from Myers-Briggs, more people prefer introversion than extroversion, yet the societal bias towards extroversion conditions many introverts to undervalue themselves.

This chapter addresses these limiting beliefs, emphasizing that low self-confidence is not an inherent trait of introversion but a result of societal conditioning.

By elevating their self-belief, introverted entrepreneurs can unlock their full potential. They learn to leverage their unique strengths—deep thinking, introspection, strong listening skills—and build self-belief.

This transformation is not just about individual success but about embracing and valuing diversity in entrepreneurial traits.

It empowers introverts to achieve their dreams, proving that self-belief is a powerful catalyst for turning entrepreneurial visions into reality.

Embracing your introversion as a superpower can lead to incredible success, as shown through personal stories and research.

With practical strategies and studying the success of other well-known introverted entrepreneurs, you will be able to recognize beliefs that diminish your self-worth, challenge them, and harness your natural strengths. By doing so, you can navigate the entrepreneurial landscape with confidence, authenticity, and a renewed sense of purpose.

Low self-confidence isn't an inherent trait of introversion. It's a limiting belief.

Beth Buelow, author of "The Introvert Entrepreneur" shares that "Self-confidence is one of the most important ingredients for success, but it's often one of the biggest challenges for introverts."

I found this to be true for myself and in onboarding conversations with my coaching clients. Simply stated, low self-confidence isn't an inherent trait of introversion. It's a limiting belief.

When it comes to the power of self-belief and how crucial it is to achieving success in both entrepreneurship and in life, a study published in the Journal of Business Venturing Insights found that entrepreneurs with higher levels of self-confidence are associated with better entrepreneurial success (Maczulskij & Viinikainen, 2023).

Another study published by the Journal of Entrepreneurship Education concluded that entrepreneurs who have a high self-belief show greater intellectual ability, strategic flexibility, are able to adapt to changes in plans and manage environmental fluctuations (Garaika, et al, 2019).

How do you elevate your self-belief as an introverted entrepreneur? First, recognize that being an introvert doesn't mean you're automatically lacking what it takes.

In the CEO Genome Project it was revealed that while boards are often impressed by charismatic extroverts, introverts are more likely to exceed the expectations of their boards and investors.

Next, embrace your natural introverted strengths.

Second, identify and challenge limiting beliefs related to self-belief. Once identified, question the validity. "Is this based on facts or assumptions?"

Third, break down large goals into manageable tasks and

celebrate accomplishments. This practice builds momentum and reinforces your belief in your capabilities.

Releasing limiting beliefs

An often overlooked, but powerful component when it comes to elevating your self-belief as an introverted entrepreneur is to have support and accountability in the form of a coach, mentor or accountability group.

Remember, as an introverted entrepreneur, your introverted strengths are an asset - particularly the ability to be introspective, however do consider another viewpoint can be an accelerator to the transformation you desire.

One of my coaching clients, Debbie Clason, CEO of Clason Communication shared this, "I was downsized from a successful career as a Marketing Specialist and decided to put my skills to work by starting my own business. Even though I had experienced great success in my corporate role, I found myself paralyzed by a lack of confidence and belief in my abilities as an entrepreneurial introvert. I struggled my first two years. By working with Stephanie and her coaching framework I was able to raise my level of self-belief and experienced a steady increase in my business income."

Essentially, releasing limiting beliefs liberates the introvert to unapologetically cultivate the very qualities - such as focus, creativity, active listening and perceptive observation - that are invaluable entrepreneurial assets when leveraged effectively.

Elevating self-belief as an introverted entrepreneur involves recognizing and overcoming limiting beliefs, leveraging your strengths, and continuously working on personal growth.

By understanding that low self-confidence is not an inherent trait of introversion, but a limiting belief, you can unlock your true potential and achieve more entrepreneurial success. Remember, self-belief is a powerful catalyst for turning your entrepreneurial dreams into reality.

Your 30-Day Challenge
30-Day Self-Belief Action Plan

1. Morning Check-In:
Write in a journal to assess your initial level of confidence.

Questions to Answer:

◆ How confident do I feel today on a scale from 1 to 10?
◆ What thoughts or feelings are contributing to this level of confidence?
◆ Is there anything specific I am looking forward to or dreading today?

2. Evening Check-In:
Reflect on your day and record your level of confidence at the end of the day.

Questions to Answer:

◆ How confident do I feel now on a scale from 1 to 10?
◆ What events, interactions, or thoughts influenced my confidence today?
◆ Were there any moments when my confidence significantly increased or decreased? Why?

3. Weekly:

Review your daily check-ins and look for patterns or trends in your confidence levels and ask yourself:

- ◆ What situations consistently boost my confidence?
- ◆ What situations consistently lower my confidence?

4. Twice during the 30 days (Day 1 and Day 15)

1. Analyze how your environment impacts your confidence.

2. Internal Environment: Reflect on your thoughts, self-talk, and emotional state.

3. External Environment: Consider the people, places, and situations around you.

Questions to Answer:

- ◆ How does my internal environment affect my confidence?
- ◆ How does my external environment influence my confidence?

Get 7 powerful strategies to create a reserve of self-belief so you can create the results you want in your business and life: www.GetYourMindOnYourSide.com

About the Author

Stephanie is the founder of LiveWire Coaching & Consulting. Her 30+ year professional career includes a diversity of technical roles, industry experience, leadership responsibility, credentials and client success stories.

As a success strategist, and empowerment coach, Stephanie uses her proven framework to coach and mentor introverted quiet achievers. She helps them embrace how they are wired and empowers them to achieve more financial independence, success and significance on their terms.

Along with her background in engineering, corporate leadership, executive coaching and business, Stephanie is a mentor, thought leader, keynote speaker, podcast guest, best-selling author and featured industry leader in the best-seller, 'Selling From Your Comfort Zone' by Stacey Hall.

Stephanie Y. Oden
LiveWire Coaching & Consulting
questions@stephanieoden.com
https://www.linkedin.com/in/stephanieyoden/

"I'm not going to limit myself just because people won't accept the fact that I can do something else."

— Dolly Parton

DR. PATRICIA SUGGS

Dedication
To my husband, Doug who is always there for me and to
women 55+ who aren't close to being done in the workplace

CHAPTER 4

HOW TO OPEN THE GLASS DOORS TO MORE PROMOTIONS AND RAISES

By Dr. Patricia Suggs

Coming face-to-face with glass doors

Opening glass doors can be a challenge for women 55+, but not impossible. Women 55+ have so much wisdom, talent and experiences; however, many are passed over for raises and promotions in favor of younger men and women. According to a survey done by AARP in 2021, 78% of women ages 50-64 experienced ageism. The time is now for women 55+ to stand up and speak out, revealing their wisdom and wealth of experience and value to the workplace.

For women 55+ it is crucial for them to continue to grow and enhance their skills in order to still be in the game for promotions and raises. Research has shown that women over 50 are more likely to be pushed aside in favor of younger women. The 30 Days Guide will bring the transformation of awareness of the key tools in conflict reconciliation and how these tools can be used in all important conversations, not just conflict, and will increase your visibility to all those around you. With these tools women 55+ will increase their self-confidence and be at ease when talking with everyone including CEOs and supervisors. This confidence will enable them to stand up for themselves and become more visible in the workplace. These tools will enable them to communicate better with all generations and become key players within teams.

Overall, the ability to reconcile conflicts empowers professional women 55+ to navigate challenges effectively, build successful working relationships, and contribute positively to the dynamic landscape of today's workplaces.

Glass doors can present challenges and opportunities for women 55+

Understanding and embodying the skills of Conflict Reconciliation are important in opening the glass doors. Glass doors can present challenges and opportunities to women 55+. The skill to handle any conversation effectively is a key to great leadership. These key tools help women 55+ reclaim any confidence that may have dimmed and achieve the success that they desire. Two points to remember:

◆ Effective conflict reconciliation can help in building stronger, more positive relationships with colleagues, subordinates, and supervisors, reducing workplace stress and improving overall morale.

◆ Developing conflict reconciliation skills is an enhanced leadership skill. It can improve the ability to manage and lead teams and foster a more collaborative and productive work environment.

Before moving forward, you must begin the process with yourself and do it with heart. What do you want to come out of the conversation? How do you want to present yourself?

And then you have to ask yourself questions such as: 'What are my triggers?' 'How do I typically react to conflict?' 'What are some reasons I react the way I do?' 'Where did I learn my response to conflict?' 'How do I really want to deal with conflict situations?'

Once you have this personal awareness then there are 5 key tools/strategies that are critical to deal with conflict reconciliation effectively. They are: Presence, Nonjudgment, Deep Listening, Powerful Questions, and Accountability.

These skills are transformative. They will get you noticed and on your way to offers of promotions and raises.

Younger is not always better

Many businesses refuse to see the great value in their women 55+ employees. Most believe that younger is better, disregarding the vast experience and wisdom that this group has.

After researching the topic of women 55+, I found there is very little research in this area at all. Women 55+ are still seeking to move through the glass doors (barriers to promotions and raises). Bonnie Marcus wrote a book "Not Done Yet" published in 2021. This is the only recent source I have found that talks plainly about the challenges for women 55+. Her philosophy is that women over 50 must debunk the myths that they may deeply harbor, such as 'I am too old to get promoted,' 'I am too old to compete,' I am irrelevant,' 'I am not attractive enough.' She lays out her recommendations clearly and concisely. They include: love yourself; put yourself first; choose the glass half full. Amen to all of these.

Other than Marcus, I found no recent research on helping

women 55+ continue to pursue their dreams and goals, whether it is to open more glass doors, exit from current employment, or to establish their own business.

I believe there is one specific area not covered in Marcus' book. In order to be noticed, women 55+ must come out of the shadows and have the skills that help them in the area of conflict reconciliation. With these skills you are more confident and able to handle any situation. And you will be noticed!

Non-anxious presence is the art of showing neutrality

The solution that I offer works. I know this because it worked for me and others I have coached. With a great deal of practice, non-anxious presence is the art of showing neutrality in one's face and body language. It is the ability to remain neutral on the outside, even in the midst of anger and upset, which enables conversations to happen calmly. It takes practice because we typically show what we're feeling. Non-judgment means throwing away assumptions and being totally present to those in front of me. Deep Listening is listening with the intent to hear exactly what the person is saying to you. This technique is used in the coaching field. Only with deep listening, added with curiosity, can you come up with powerful questions. Powerful questions come from deep listening, because when you know what the person means, then your curiosity will produce the questions that need answering. Accountability is being accountable to myself (am I present, am I really listening, am I asking the right questions and am I being accountable), and if you have a trusted colleague, letting them hold you accountable is a great benefit.

When I, and those I coach, practice these concepts over and

over again, we notice a transformation taking place, both inside and out. We feel more confident in our leadership and know we can handle any situation.

When I have coached others in the process, they have all come away with a heightened sense of confidence and self-assurance. Conflict or disagreements didn't frighten them anymore. This is not to say that difficult conversations can't still be anxiety producing, however, you won't be showing it in your face or demeanor.

For women 55+ this transformation will open the glass doors and you will be successful.

Your 30-Day Challenge

The 30 Days Guide will give the knowledge needed to understand and embody the tools/skills of Conflict Reconciliation. Journal your conversations each week and give your insights, did you notice differences in the ways you understood others? Were there AHA moments?

Week 1: Non-anxious Presence. The ability to put on a neutral but interested face and body language when talking with others, especially in any type of disagreement. Embody this concept and practice at work with everyone you talk to.

Week 2: Non-judgment and Deep Listening. Go into any conversation with no judgment or prior assumptions. Truly listen to someone and hear what they say and mean. Repeat back to them if necessary before moving forward with the conversation.

Week 3: Powerful Questions. When you really hear the meaning of what someone is saying, you will find that questions come to mind easily. The more you practice the easier it will become. Don't ask unnecessary questions, only those that are pertinent to the conversation.

Week 4: Accountability. Hold yourself accountable, by reflecting on all of your conversations. Were you present? Did you go in with no judgment and truly listen? Did you ask powerful questions? If in a group conversation with a trusted colleague, have them hold you accountable with the above questions.

By the end of the 30 days, you will understand what it takes to open the glass door. You will see a transformation within yourself, an awareness of the skills that are essential for your success.

"How to Master Receiving Recognition from Your Boss" recorded training program included with your 15-minute no-charge Recognition Strategy Session. Book your session here: https://calendly.com/patricia-arise/transformationdiscovery-call

About the Author

Dr. Patricia Suggs is a Conflict Reconciliation Expert and "What's Next" Strategist, who supports professional women leaders 55+ to pass through the glass doors that often hinder them from receiving promotions and raises. She provides training to strengthen and enhance their leadership skills including: self-confidence; imposter syndrome; self-sabotage; and conflict reconciliation to achieve their passions and goals.

Dr. Suggs has an extensive educational background: M.Div., M.Ed., Ph.D. and certifications in Coaching, Conflict Reconciliation and Healing Touch. Her speaking experience spans over 40 years and she is a #1 global best-selling author covering important topics for professional women. Her experiences include lead pastor of several churches, Associate Professor in Geriatrics at Wake Forest University School of Medicine, working with groups and individuals for education and training in conflict reconciliation and helping groups work through difficult/conflict situations. She has been coaching/consulting for over 15 years and 2 years ago started ARISE Leadership Consulting, LLC.

Dr. Patricia Suggs
ARISE Leadership Consulting, LLC
patricia@pksuggscoaching.net
www.linkedin.com/in/drpatriciasuggs

DORTHA HISE

Dedication
To entrepreneurs and executives who working and are
available "24/7" seeking a better way...
you can do this!

CHAPTER 5

RECLAIM 4 HOURS PER WEEK – THAT'S 192 HOURS PER YEAR!

By Dortha Hise, BSc, BA, C. Graphic Design

How Time and Processes Can Be an Entrepreneur's Kryptonite

Entrepreneurs are the face of their business. And they tend to feel the need to be "on" all the time, leading to chronic overextension and feelings of burnout, especially among high-achieving entrepreneurial and executive women. These women often feel responsible to wear all of the hats in the business, and ultimately that leads to micromanagement and an inability to take time off. This guide dismantles the belief that their business will fail without their constant oversight.

Through a strategic and easy approach to delegation and time-management, the guide helps women reclaim at least 4 hours each week—16 hours a month, or two full business days. This time can be redirected to strategic planning, personal well-being, or quality time with loved ones. The 30-day challenge encourages small, incremental changes that lead to significant improvements in work-life balance.

The challenge provides practical steps for identifying tasks that can be delegated, tasks that are essential personal tasks, and high-level strategic activities. It introduces tools and techniques for effective project management, ensuring clear communication, and setting realistic expectations within teams.

Additionally, the challenge fosters a mindset shift, encouraging women to trust their teams and accept that mistakes are part of the growth process. By letting go of perfectionism, they can empower their team members and build a culture of trust and autonomy, which alleviates their burden and enhances team performance and business efficiency.

This guide aims to solve the problem of unsustainable workloads and the fear of taking time off, helping entrepreneurs to lead more balanced, productive, and fulfilled lives.

Why does solving this problem matter?

Let's face it – solving the chronic overextension and burnout among high-achieving entrepreneurial and executive women is crucial for multiple reasons.

First, persistent micromanagement and the inability to delegate effectively lead to significant stress, sleep issues, relationship challenges, and more. These women often feel they cannot step away because the business cannot run without them, and this adds to their stress levels and diminishes their overall mental wellness. Addressing this problem helps prevent burnout, allowing them to maintain their health and vitality. I have also found that clients experience a higher degree of satisfaction in their business as result of delegating more because it allows them to get back to the things they love doing in their business.

Second, the inability to take time off stifles creativity and strategic thinking. Constantly being in the operational trenches leaves little room for big-picture planning or innovative thinking, which are essential for business growth and sustainability. By reclaiming time through effective delegation and intentional scheduling, these leaders can focus on strategic initiatives that drive their businesses forward.

Furthermore, solving this problem is vital for fostering a positive organizational culture. When leaders trust their teams and delegate effectively, it empowers the team, enhances their satisfaction, and boosts morale. A culture of trust and autonomy leads to higher productivity, better retention rates, and a more resilient organization.

Addressing this issue also has profound personal benefits.

High-achieving women often sacrifice personal time and relationships for their careers. Reclaiming even a few hours a week can significantly improve their work-life balance, allowing for more meaningful connections with family and friends and opportunities for personal growth and self-care.

In essence, solving the problem of overextension and burnout is critical because it leads to healthier, more innovative, and sustainable business practices. It also enhances personal well-being, improves organizational culture, and fosters an environment where both leaders and their teams can thrive.

Why is this issue still not solved you ask?

In a few ways - one is that it isn't being solved. Entrepreneurs and executive women wear so many hats in their business, and it is almost an expectation that they "figure it all out." Next, in her doctoral dissertation, Dr. Carolina Billings uncovered that women were spending tons of time using ChatGPT for simple things... like composing a post for a social media channel. The bigger things, women were not utilizing ChatGPT for.

The bottom line is that tend to gravitate toward automating the *simple* things - in the grand scheme, did it really save time? No.

Research, Social Proof, and Case Studies

The solutions utilized in my business have come from 20 years of experience, a combination of research, social proof, and case studies suggest that effective delegation, combined with strategic scheduling led to happier clients.

Research indicates that effective delegation and time management practices lead to improved productivity, reduced stress, and greater work-life balance. Studies show that team members with high levels of autonomy and well-being are more productive and contribute to better organizational outcomes. (Sources: https://ijsrmst.com/index.php/ijsrmst/article/view/113/108 and https://ijrrt.com/index.php/ijrrt/article/view/58/29)

Furthermore, social proof from satisfied clients validates the efficacy of the approach. Case studies from our business showcase tangible transformations achieved by our clients.

For instance, Ann*, initially came to me incredibly overwhelmed and stressed, not to mention missing quality time with her spouse. Through coaching with me, she successfully reclaimed time for her passion—yoga—leading to improved relationships and work-life balance. Another client, Sharon*, recognized the need for delegation to elevate her business to the next level, ultimately achieving her goal of vacationing with her partner.

And lastly, Maria knew that she needed the support of an effective team, yet was afraid of relinquishing control of things in her business. Through working together with me, she discovered the magic of intentional and strategic scheduling provided her to the opportunity to pursue her dream of writing a book while effectively managing her business responsibilities.

These case studies provide concrete evidence of our solution's impact on clients' lives and businesses. Their success stories highlight the tangible results achieved through effective delegation and intentional time management strategies. By leveraging research findings and real-world testimonials, we are confident in the effectiveness of our solution in helping high-achieving women reclaim time, reduce stress, and achieve greater fulfillment in both their personal and professional lives.

*Names have been changed to protect privacy

30-Day Challenge: Intentional Scheduling

Intentional scheduling and fostering trust within your team are the keys to unlocking the freedom to take time off without sacrificing productivity or peace of mind.

By following the weekly exercises provided on the following pages, you will gradually streamline your workflow, delegate tasks effectively, and prioritize high-value activities.

Week 1: Assess and Delegate

◆ Step 1: Write out everything you do in your business.

◆ Step 2: Identify tasks that can be delegated to others.

◆ Step 3: Create a color-coded system to distinguish between essential tasks and those that can be delegated.

◆ Step 4: Start small by delegating one task this week and track the results.

Week 2: Prioritize and Schedule

◆ Step 1: Prioritize your tasks based on importance and urgency.

◆ Step 2: Categorize tasks into CEO-level responsibilities and tasks that can be handled by others.

◆ Step 3: Schedule time blocks for CEO-level tasks and delegate the rest.

◆ Step 4: Review your schedule daily and make adjustments as needed to stay on track.

Week 3: Build Trust and Clear Communication

◆ Step 1: Set clear expectations with your team regarding delegated tasks.

◆ Step 2: Establish open lines of communication for feedback and updates.

◆ Step 3: Encourage autonomy and decision-making among team members.

◆ Step 4: Foster a culture of trust by acknowledging and appreciating the efforts of your team.

Week 4: Self-Care and Reflection

◆ Step 1: Schedule regular self-care activities such as exercise, hobbies, or time with loved ones.

◆ Step 2: Reflect on your progress throughout the challenge.

◆ Step 3: Celebrate your successes and identify areas for further improvement.

◆ Step 4: Create a plan to maintain your newfound balance and continue reclaiming your time in the future.

These weekly steps will guide you to reclaiming your valuable time, as well as cultivate a sustainable approach to managing your schedule and delegating tasks effectively. Remember, it's all about taking small, intentional steps towards a more balanced and fulfilling life. Be gentle with yourself in the process and remember that practice makes progress as we traverse the Summit to Your Success!

Book your discovery call to explore more ways to take strategic and intentional scheduling to the next level and the next steps in reclaiming your time: https://form.jotform.com/dortha/say-yes-to-balance

About the Author

Dortha L. Hise is a multifaceted individual, celebrated International Bestselling Author, and the ingenious mind behind Summit to Your Success, a pioneering coaching and project management firm dedicated to liberating clients from overwhelm.

She leads clients to transformative experiences in their life and business by harnessing the healing power of nature. Dortha's own journey, marked by resilience and triumph over adversity, fuels her passion for empowering high achievers to transcend limitations and optimize their businesses for peak performance.

Her firsthand experience with Abductor Spasmodic Dysphonia, a neurological condition, heightened her capacity for deep listening—a skill she employs to facilitate profound mindset shifts and personal transformations in her coaching practice.

Drawing from her first transformative 3-day backpacking excursion, Dortha channels strategic and intuitive techniques to instigate powerful shifts in perception and behavior. Dortha is a certified coach empowering her clients to efficiency in their business, she is unwavering in her commitment to equipping leaders with the tools they need to serve the world at their best, guiding them towards a future defined by clarity, purpose, and boundless potential.

Dortha Hise, BSc, BA, C. Graphic Design
Summit to Your Success
dortha@summittoyoursuccess.com
https://www.linkedin.com/in/dorthahise/

"My mission in life is not merely to survive, but to thrive."
— Maya Angelou

DR. CAROLINA M. BILLINGS

Dedication

To my father, Dr. Carlos Munoz Barillas, whose every word guides me to this day.

CHAPTER 6
30 DAYS TO ESTABLISHING YOURSELF AS A LINKEDIN SUBJECT MATTER EXPERT

By Dr. Carolina M. Billings

Visibility and digital footprint are crucial to personal branding, networking, thought leadership, access to opportunities, reputation management, and democratizing access to expertise. By strategically managing your online presence, you can enhance your professional and personal development, contributing globally to your fields and society.

LinkedIn Influencer and LinkedIn Marketing is a real thing

LinkedIn, once primarily for job seekers and business experts, has evolved into a hub for professional influencers open to mutually beneficial collaborations with business owners. LinkedIn influencer marketing now leverages Subject Matter Experts with significant followings and expertise to boost brand awareness, sales, reach, trust, and credibility. To elevate your small business, explore LinkedIn influencer marketing, including its benefits and best collaboration practices with LinkedIn professionals.

Discover how to harness this powerful strategy for your business growth. What kind of LinkedIn influencer are you?

Nano influencers: These are influencers with less than 10k followers. They are far less professional than other influencers and tend to post typical content on their page.

Micro-influencers: These are influences with 10k-50k followers. They generally get the most genuine engagement compared to other influencers.

Mid-tier influencers: These are influencers with 50k-500k followers, and they also tend to get genuine engagement.

Macro influencers: These are influencers with 500k-1M followers. They generally have wider experience in different topics and can therefore reach a wider net.

Mega influencers: These are influencers with more than 1M followers. But don't let their extensive following base fool you—their engagement isn't always as high as their following.

Source: LinkedIn.com

Why LinkedIn?

Here are the top reasons why using a platform like LinkedIn is your fastest way to establishing your credibility as an expert:

Personal Branding and Career Advancement

Problem: In a highly competitive market, individuals face the challenge of differentiating themselves from others with similar qualifications and experience.

Why it matters:

◆ **Visibility:** By cultivating a strong digital presence through platforms like LinkedIn, personal blogs, and social media, individuals can highlight their expertise, showcase their achievements, and demonstrate thought leadership. This can lead to greater recognition and opportunities for career advancement.

◆ **Digital Footprint:** A well-managed digital footprint serves as a portfolio that employers, clients, and collaborators can review, providing evidence of skills, accomplishments, and professional development.

Network Building and Knowledge Exchange

Problem: Traditional methods of networking and knowledge exchange can be limited by geographical and institutional boundaries, reducing opportunities for collaboration and innovation.

Why it matters:

◆ **Visibility:** Online platforms and digital visibility break down these barriers, allowing individuals to connect with a global audience. This fosters relationships with peers, mentors, and potential collaborators across the world.

◆ **Digital Footprint:** Engaging in online communities, contributing to discussions, and sharing research and ideas enhance one's visibility and credibility, facilitating richer knowledge exchange and collaborative opportunities.

Thought Leadership and Influence

Problem: Establishing oneself as a thought leader requires consistent dissemination of ideas and insights to a broad audience, which is difficult to achieve through traditional publishing channels alone.

Why it matters:

◆ **Visibility:** Through blogs, social media, and participation in online forums, individuals can share their insights and research more broadly and frequently, influencing public discourse and academic debates.

◆ **Digital Footprint:** A substantial digital footprint, marked by high-quality content and active engagement, positions an individual as a credible and influential voice in their field, attracting followers, invitations to speak, and opportunities to influence policy and practice.

Access to Opportunities and Resources

Problem: Many opportunities for funding, collaboration, and professional development are increasingly discovered and secured online.

Why it matters:

◆ **Visibility:** Being visible in digital spaces increases the likelihood of encountering and being considered for such opportunities. Funders, employers, and collaborators often search for candidates with a robust online presence.

◆ **Digital Footprint:** A comprehensive digital footprint, showcasing a history of successful projects and collaborations, can serve as a testament to one's capability and reliability, enhancing access to resources and opportunities.

Information and Reputation Management

Problem: Misinformation, negative feedback, or lack of information can harm an individual›s reputation and professional prospects.

Why it matters:

◆ **Visibility:** Active management of one's digital presence allows for immediate and positive engagement with audiences, mitigating negative information and promoting accurate, favorable content.

◆ **Digital Footprint:** A well-curated digital footprint acts as a defence mechanism, presenting a consistent and positive narrative that can outweigh isolated negative incidents or misinformation.

Democratizing Access to Expertise and Insights

Problem: Traditional gatekeeping in academia and industry often restricts access to valuable knowledge and expertise to a select few.

Why it matters:

◆ **Visibility:** By leveraging digital platforms, experts can democratize access to their knowledge, making it available to a wider audience, including those who may not have access through traditional means.

◆ **Digital Footprint:** This broad dissemination of expertise and insights contributes to a more informed and educated public, fostering innovation and informed decision-making across various sectors.

So why most people are still getting LinkedIn so wrong?

While the concepts of visibility and digital footprint are widely discussed, there are several common misconceptions and pitfalls that people often encounter when trying to leverage these tools for personal and professional growth. Here are some key misunderstandings:

Overemphasis on Quantity Over Quality

Misconception: More content and frequent posts are always better for visibility.

Reality: Quality trumps quantity. Posting frequently but with low-quality content can dilute your brand and reduce your credibility. Thoughtful, well-crafted content that adds value to your audience is more effective in building a strong digital footprint.

Ignoring Audience Engagement

Misconception: Simply having a digital presence is enough to be visible and influential.

Reality: Engagement is crucial. Passive presence without interaction does not build relationships or a loyal following.

Responding to comments, participating in discussions, and actively engaging with your audience is essential for creating meaningful connections and enhancing visibility.

Underestimating the Importance of Consistency

Misconception: Inconsistent or sporadic activity on digital platforms is sufficient as long as the content is good.

Reality: Consistency builds trust and keeps your audience engaged. Regular updates and interactions help maintain visibility and ensure that you remain top of mind for your audience. Inconsistent activity can lead to audience attrition and reduced impact.

Focusing Solely on Self-Promotion

Misconception: Digital visibility is all about self-promotion and highlighting personal achievements.

Reality: While self-promotion is important, providing value to your audience through educational, informative, or entertaining content is equally crucial. Focusing solely on self-promotion can be off-putting and may alienate your audience.

Neglecting Privacy and Security

Misconception: Maximizing visibility means sharing as much as possible about yourself online.

Reality: Balancing visibility with privacy and security is essential. Over-sharing personal information can lead to privacy breaches and other security issues. It›s important to be strategic about what you share and to protect sensitive information.

Assuming Digital Presence Equals Expertise

Misconception: A strong digital footprint automatically establishes someone as an expert.

Reality: While a digital footprint can enhance perceived expertise, it must be backed by actual knowledge, experience, and credibility. Inflating your credentials or pretending to be an expert without the requisite background can backfire and damage your reputation.

Overlooking the Power of Analytics

Misconception: Success in digital visibility cannot be measured effectively.

Reality: Analytics tools can provide valuable insights into what works and what doesn›t in your digital strategy. Ignoring analytics means missing out on opportunities to optimize your approach based on real data.

Neglecting Platform-Specific Strategies

Misconception: One-size-fits-all content works across all digital platforms.

Reality: Different platforms cater to different audiences and have unique norms and best practices. Tailoring your content to fit the specific platform is critical for maximizing impact and engagement.

Believing Digital Footprint is Permanent and Unchangeable

Misconception: Once something is online, it can never be changed or improved.

Reality: While it›s true that digital content can be persistent, proactive steps can be taken to manage and improve your digital footprint over time. Regularly updating profiles, correcting misinformation, and adding new, positive content can help shape your online presence.

Overlooking Offline Integration

Misconception: Digital visibility alone is enough to achieve professional success.

Reality: Combining online visibility with offline networking and real-world interactions is often the most effective strategy. Offline credibility can enhance your digital presence, and vice versa.

**Your first 30-Day Challenge toward your
ultimate Profile with Visibility and Impact.**

Your ultimate goal is to create a Top 1% LinkedIn profile with several key elements that can significantly enhance your professional presence and attract the right opportunities. Here are four essential components:

1. Compelling Headline and Profile Summary

Headline:

◆ **Clear and Concise:** Your headline should quickly convey who you are and what you do. Avoid just listing your job title; highlight your key skills or unique value proposition. For example, instead of "Marketing Manager," use "Digital Marketing Expert | SEO Specialist | Content Strategist."

Profile Summary:

◆ **Engaging and Informative:** Your summary should provide a snapshot of your professional journey, key accomplishments, and what you bring to the table. Use a conversational tone, include relevant keywords, and make sure it reflects your personality and professional brand.

◆ **Call to Action:** End your summary with a call to action, inviting readers to connect, visit your website, or check out your portfolio.

2. Professional Photo and Background Image

Profile Photo:

◆ **High-Quality:** Use a professional, high-resolution photo where you are dressed appropriately for your industry. Ensure good lighting and a neutral background to keep the focus on you.

◆ **Approachable:** Smile and look approachable, as this can make a positive first impression and encourage connections.

Background Image aka Banner:

◆ **Relevant and Eye-Catching:** Use a background image that represents your industry, your personal brand, or your interests. This can be a custom graphic, a relevant stock photo, or a branded image that adds visual interest to your profile.

3. Detailed Experience and Achievements

Experience Section:

◆ **Specific and Quantifiable:** Detail your job roles with specific responsibilities, projects, and achievements. Use bullet points for readability and quantify your achievements with numbers and metrics where possible

◆ **Storytelling:** Instead of just listing tasks, explain the impact you made in each role. For example, "Increased sales by 30% through targeted marketing campaigns" is more impactful than "Responsible for sales."

Achievements:

◆ **Highlight Key Milestones:** Include any awards, recognitions, or significant accomplishments. This adds credibility and demonstrates your expertise and success in your field.

4. Skills, Endorsements, and Recommendations

Skills:

◆ **Relevant Skills:** List skills that are most relevant to your industry and career goals. Ensure the top skills listed are those you want to be recognized for.

◆ **Endorsements:** Regularly update your skills and seek

endorsements from colleagues and connections to build credibility.

Recommendations:

◆ **Genuine and Specific:** Request recommendations from colleagues, supervisors, or clients who can speak to your strengths and contributions. Personalized, specific recommendations are more impactful than generic ones.

◆ **Balanced Perspective:** Aim to have recommendations that reflect different aspects of your professional abilities, such as leadership, teamwork, and technical skills.

Final Thought

A LinkedIn profile combines a compelling headline and summary, professional photos, detailed experience and achievements, and robust skills and endorsements. By focusing on these elements, you can create a profile that effectively showcases your professional brand, attracts the right opportunities, and builds valuable connections.

Join our LinkedIn Empowerment Circle! Enhance your visibility, connect with industry leaders, and amplify your impact. Collaborate, share insights, and grow together. Elevate your professional presence—join us today and transform your LinkedIn experience. https://powerful-women-today.mn.co/share/N-RI6klKX1mH5haM?utm_source=manual

About the Author

Dr. Carolina M. Billings, Ph.D., MA-IS, CHRL, SHRP-SCP, CPCC is a social impact entrepreneur with 15+ years of Corporate C-Suite leadership experience. As a former CFO/CHRO Dr. Billings specializes in Strategic Growth, bringing professional accreditations, practical experience and scientific research in the fields of Business Development, Leadership, Branding, Human Resources and Finance.

Dr. Billings is the founder of Powerful Women Today, a boutique accelerator for women's success. A forum for the empowerment and optimization of women's status and lives. Her Ph.D. Dissertation: The Impact of Generative AI, Technology and Marketing Aggregates, is the culmination of empirical research based on the Research Pilot: Powerful Women Today PWT10X Activating 10 key accelerators for entrepreneurial success.

Her Boutique Management Consulting Firm is comprised of elite experts championing women's growth, Her Academy, Book and Magazine Multi- Media Publishing Division and Global Network continuously innovate removing barriers to entry and success. She aims to positively impact 1 Million Women every year to champion their emotional and financial independence.

Dr. Carolina M. Billings
Ph.D., MA-IS, SHRP-SCP, CHRL, CPP, CPCC
Powerful Women Today
info@powerfulwomentoday.com
https://www.linkedin.com/in/drcarolinambillings/

"Well-behaved women seldom make history."
— Laurel Thatcher Ulrich

Part 2: Self

RAJIKA MAHAN

Dedication
To my husband and my kids

CHAPTER 7

THE POWER OF YOUR SELF IMAGE

By Rajika Mahan

The true impact of Low Self-Image

The impact of a low self-image extends far beyond missed opportunities; it stifles personal growth and hinders one's ability to make meaningful contributions. When individuals, particularly women, struggle with low self-esteem, they find themselves trapped in a cycle of self-doubt and negativity preventing them from pursuing opportunities leading to a life constrained by fear and insecurity.

Low self-image affects every facet of life, from career choices to personal relationships. It can lead to underperformance at work due to a lack of confidence. The fear of failure or judgment often overshadows their capabilities, causing them to settle for less than they are capable of achieving.

In personal relationships, low self-esteem can result in settling for less than one deserves, tolerating unhealthy dynamics, and struggling to assert one's needs and desires. Individuals with low self-esteem may find themselves in relationships that do not nurture or respect them, simply because they do not believe they deserve better. This can lead to a cycle of dependency and acceptance of negative behaviors from partners, which further reinforces their low self-worth.

Additionally, low self-esteem can hinder social interactions, making it difficult to form and maintain meaningful friendships. The constant fear of judgment and rejection can cause individuals to withdraw from social situations, leading to isolation and loneliness. This lack of social support further exacerbates feelings of inadequacy and unworthiness.

Ultimately, low self-esteem limits personal and professional growth, damages relationships, and traps individuals in a cycle of negativity and self-doubt, preventing them from realizing and achieving their true potential.

Altering How We Perceive Ourselves

Shifting self-image is crucial because it fundamentally alters how we perceive ourselves and our capabilities, impacting every aspect of our lives. A positive self-image fosters confidence, love and embracing the spirit inside of each of us.

As we change our self-image it supports us in our goals, aspirations and we can make decisions and choices in harmony with ourselves.

If we don't solve these patterns, we are constantly running on a hamster wheel and never moving forward on our path. Without a positive self-image, self-doubt feels like constant frustration weighing us down.

As we undo and shift our self-image we let go of the barriers holding us back. We allow ourselves to stretch like a rubber band to explore our capacity and capabilities. By developing a healthier self-perception, we can replace these negative patterns with a more empowered and confident approach to life.

The benefits of a positive self-image extend into our professional and personal lives. In the workplace, increased self-confidence can lead to better performance, greater willingness to take risks, and more assertive communication. It supports individuals in articulating their ideas, pursuing leadership roles, and contributing more effectively to their teams.

On a more personal level, a positive self-image enhances our relationships by fostering better communication, reducing the need for external validation, and promotes respect and understanding.

Ultimately, shifting our self-image matters because it is the foundation of our self-worth and we self-love.

Are current methods still working at addressing this issue?

Research has shown that changing our self-image impacts our emotional, spiritual, mental and physical self.

Research by Dr. Kristin Neff, a leading expert in self-compassion, highlights how self-compassion practices can significantly enhance self-image. Neff's studies demonstrate that self-compassion, which involves treating oneself with kindness and understanding during times of failure or difficulty, is linked to higher self-esteem and emotional resilience. Individuals with high self-compassion are less likely to engage in self-criticism and more likely to maintain a positive self-image, which supports better mental health and life satisfaction.

Joseph Murphy was a prolific writer and lecturer who focused on the power of the subconscious mind and its impact on self-image and personal success. His work is particularly well-known for its emphasis on the mental and spiritual aspects of self-improvement, as outlined in his seminal book, "The Power of Your Subconscious Mind." While Murphy's approach blends psychological principles with a more metaphysical perspective, his insights have influenced many in the field of self-help and personal development.

The Proof is in the Results.

https://positivepsychology.com/self-esteem-research
https://www.ncbi.nlm.nih.gov/pmc/articles/PMC9306298

As an example, I share my experience of supporting one of my clients, whose low self-esteem was impacting her health, her work and her personal relationships. We started to focus on improving her belief system by identifying how she had adopted this low self-image pattern.

She shared that she was always told that "she wouldn't add up to anything". Through my process of re-framing this false belief she started to take small baby steps in her perspective with her relationships and her work. She began being known as a leader at work. In fact, a dream she had to lead a group at work for "neurodivergent" women became a reality and she received raving feedback and is now in charge of bringing change for everyone in the company.

I am inviting you to practice over the next 30 days the same process I taught to my client.

Days 1-10: Building Awareness and Foundation.

Goal: Increase self-awareness and establish a positive self-image.

Daily Journaling: Reflect on your current self-image and negative beliefs. Write a supportive letter to yourself highlighting your strengths.

Meditation: Practice 10 minutes of mindfulness meditation daily, focusing on your thoughts without judgment.

Affirmations: Repeat affirmations like "I am worthy of love and respect" and "I am capable and strong" every morning and evening.

Days 11-20: Reinforcing Positive Beliefs and Visualization

Goal: Strengthen positive beliefs and visualize desired outcomes.

Daily Journaling: Write about three things you are grateful for each day. Reflect on past successes and how they made you feel.

Visualization: Spend 10 minutes daily visualizing your ideal self and life, imagining success and confidence.

Affirmations: Use affirmations like "I am becoming more confident every day" and "I embrace my unique qualities."

Days 21-30: Integrating Changes and Embracing Your New Self

Goal: Solidify a new self-image and integrate changes into daily life.

Daily Journaling: Reflect on changes in your self-image over the past weeks. Set specific, achievable goals for the next month.

Meditation: Continue mindfulness meditation, focusing on self-acceptance and inner peace. Practice loving-kindness meditation, sending loving thoughts to yourself and others.

Affirmations: Integrate affirmations like "I trust myself and my abilities" and "I am proud of who I am becoming" into your daily routine. *Acts of Kindness*: Perform one act of kindness each day for yourself and reflect on how these acts make you feel.

Book a 30-minute Breakthrough Session with Rajika to create a path towards clarity, confidence, and courage: https://bit.ly/35Zpciz

About the Author

Rajika Mahan is a certified Transformational Confidence and Clarity Coach, Positive Intelligence Coach, and Soma Breath Instructor. She was one of four coaches who was a finalist in the Transformational Coach of the Award 2023 at Brave Thinking Institute, Expanding her expertise, Rajika is trained as a Neurocoach with an understanding of the intricate connections between our brain and behavior.

Rajika specializes in dream-building, result acceleration, and cultivating richer, more fulfilling lives. She guides clients to break free from limitations and outdated patterns. Her approach is grounded in the understanding that true change begins with transforming our thought processes.

She was born in New Delhi, India and went to an all-girls boarding school in Jaipur. She moved to the US in 1983 with her family. She lives in Virginia with her husband and mom. She enjoys reading, watching criminal shows and horseback riding. Her ultimate vision? To empower individuals to unlock their fullest potential and thrive in every aspect of life.

Rajika Mahan
Rajika Mahan Life Coaching
rajikamahan1@gmail.com
https://www.linkedin.com/in/rajika-mahan/

"Am I good enough? Yes, I am."
— Michelle Obama

BRENDA MARTINO

Dedication

To my late husband Tony, who supported me in starting this journey to find my missing pieces, and to my son, Jacob, for continuing the support and love that his dad started. Your encouragement has helped make me whole again.

CHAPTER 8

HOW TO ELEVATE BY FINDING THE MISSING PIECES OF YOURSELF

By Brenda Martino

Who am I? The ever-changing question and answer.

Many middle-aged women talk about the feeling of not knowing who they are any more. When I was going through this, women in my circle put on a happy face and didn't talk about what was going on with them. It wasn't until I started talking about it first that a few of my friends admitted that they felt the same way. When I started to research how to solve the problem, I was surprised to discover many middle-aged women also struggle with anxiety, unhappiness, and even depression.

One of the situations we deal with is menopause, which typically occurs between the ages of 40 and 55. Symptoms include weight gain, hot flashes, sleep disturbances, and mood swings, which can be very difficult to control. The hormonal changes can also lead to anxiety or depression. Menopause is different for everyone and most doctors are not trained on helping women who are struggling with this life change. On top of the physical symptoms, menopause can create intimacy issues with our partners and create friction in our relationship.

Along with menopause, we are also experiencing a change in the roles in life that have defined us for so long. Our children have left home, most likely the job we once loved no longer gives us joy, our aging parents are requiring more of our time. All of this leaves us feeling tired, disillusioned and confused. We don't know who we are any more.

How confusion on this question can lead to disconnection.

This confusion can lead to disconnection with loved ones and dissatisfaction with work and life. Failing to address the midlife struggles with menopause and feelings of insecurities that arise as a result can have profound effects on women's physical, mental, and social health, along with economic stability. Proactive actions and support are needed to help women navigate this crucial time of life.

For many, relationships with their spouse can become strained and could lead to divorce. Life can start to feel repetitive and boring. Emotional struggles can lead to isolation and struggles with job performance or basic daily tasks.

Persistent unhappiness and stress can cause mental health disorders such as depression and anxiety. In severe cases, the lack of emotional support and coping mechanisms can lead to substance abuse or suicidal thoughts.

Economically, women struggling with unaddressed midlife issues may start missing work or have poor job performance, leading to the loss of their jobs. Losing their job can cause even more problems with getting a new job and being able to afford health insurance. Research indicates that approximately 20-30% of women in midlife experience clinical depression, which is a major contributor to health-related disabilities. Had I known there were ways to address feelings of confusion, anxiety, and depression during midlife, I would have acted immediately. It took me several years to discover these solutions on my own.

Are current solutions missing the mark?

The feelings of being lost and confused during midlife seem to be the precursor of more serious problems like depression, life-threatening diseases, metabolic syndrome, and more. Currently, women are being encouraged to have their mental health monitored during midlife, to stay fit, and possibly to consider HRT.

"Depression in the menopause transition: risks in the changing hormone milieu" -This article explores the increased prevalence of depressive symptoms during the menopause transition. It highlights how hormonal changes, particularly during perimenopause, contribute to higher rates of depression, with significant impacts on mental health. The study emphasizes the importance of addressing these hormonal influences in treatment strategies (https://womensmidlifehealthjournal. biomedcentral.com/articles/10.1186/s40695-015-0002-y)

"Since in many cases depression is a lifelong condition and is associated with severe comorbid conditions, further studies are needed to improve the early diagnosis of depression; it may be advisable to monitor a woman's mental health during the menopause transition to prevent a depressive disorder having long-term negative consequences." https://pubmed.ncbi.nlm.nih.gov/22196311/

"Midlife fitness is associated with a lower risk of later-life depression, CVD mortality, and CVD mortality after incident later-life depression. These findings suggest the importance of midlife fitness in preventing depression and subsequent CVD mortality in older age and that physicians should consider fitness and physical activity in promoting healthy aging." https://jamanetwork.com/journals/jamapsychiatry/article-abstract/2686049

"The current evidence contributes to a re-reading of the relationship between menopause and depression. The combination of the antidepressant with HT seems to offer the best therapeutic potential in terms of efficacy, rapid improvement, and consistency of remission in the follow-up.." https://pubmed.ncbi.nlm.nih.gov/19465674/

Gratitude journaling can be a powerful tool for women struggling with midlife challenges. Research shows that gratitude journaling can reduce symptoms of depression and improve overall mental and emotional health. For example, a study published in the Journal of Psychosomatic Research found that participants who engaged in gratitude exercises reported being less depressed and more optimistic about their lives (Wood et al., 2010).

How Journaling can get to the heart of the matter.

Of the various recommended solutions, I personally prefer gratitude journaling because I found it helped me find life satisfaction again.

A study in the Journal of Personality and Social Psychology found that people who kept gratitude journals experienced greater well-being and were likelier to engage in healthy behaviors, such as regular exercise and sleep (Emmons & McCullough, 2003). These behaviors are crucial for maintaining physical health, which is often challenging in midlife.

In addition to mental and physical health benefits, gratitude journaling can strengthen social relationships. Individuals who practice gratitude recognize and appreciate the support they receive from others, which is important and essential during the often confusing midlife period.

Gratitude journaling offers a simple yet effective way for those struggling with midlife challenges to improve their mental health, physical well-being, and social connections.

References:
- Wood, A. M., Froh, J. J., & Geraghty, A. W. (2010). Gratitude and well-being: A review and theoretical integration. *Clinical Psychology Review*, 30(7), 890-905.
-Emmons, R. A., & McCullough, M. E. (2003). Counting blessings versus burdens: An experimental investigation of gratitude and subjective well-being in daily life. *Journal of Personality and Social Psychology*, 84(2), 377-389.

What 30 Days of Gratitude Can do for You.

I am sharing with you my own 30-Day Gratitude Guide, which was my first step in finding my missing pieces. While most everyone has heard that gratitude practice is powerful, it remains an abstract thought to many people.

The hardest part of this Gratitude practice is it requires stillness and thought. The good news is that it can be done in as little as 5-10 minutes every day.

Week 1: Find a notebook or journal to use for this 30-day Gratitude practice. Place it on your nightstand, and each night, after you get into bed or each morning before you start your day, spend a few minutes thinking about what you are thankful for today. Then, write in the journal 1-3 things you are thankful for which happened during your day. Identify something different to appreciate each day.

Week 2: Continue the practice from Week 1 and add a statement about why you are expressing gratitude for each of them. This will help you to start feeling why you have gratitude for this person or experience.

Week 3: Continue the practice from Week 1 and Week 2 and expand to 5 items each day

Week 4: Continue the practice from Weeks 1, 2, and 3. In addition, add giving love to someone who annoys you. It is important to find something good about everyone, once you start seeing the good in them, they will stop annoying you.

The goal is to continue this Gratitude practice daily for the rest of your life. Your gratitude practice will evolve as your gratitude evolves.

8 Great Ways to Embrace Gratitude
https://d045-brenda.systeme.io/352a019c

About the Author

Brenda is a certified Transformational Coach with the DreamBuilder Program through the Brave Thinking Institute and certified coach with Proctor-Gallagher.

She is currently writing a children's book to help children who have lost a parent learn to live with their grief.

Brenda Martino
Find the Missing Piece of Yourself
brenda@brendamartino.org
https://www.linkedin.com/in/brenda-martino/

*"Courage is the price that life exacts
for granting peace."*
— Amelia Earhart

M.S. PATTERSON

Dedication

To my mentor, Yolanda Gutierrez, a woman who lived and breathed empowerment, strength, and confidence and who taught me more than I could possibly say.

CHAPTER 9

CLAIM YOUR CONFIDENCE

By M.S. Patterson

Living with a lack of confidence is not easy.

Living with a lack of confidence is not easy. Problems that arose for me (so much so that I lost sight of the fact they were problems at all) included: an inability to solve problems creatively or effectively, lack of believing in myself, being invisible in meetings and overlooked for promotion, feeling ineffective, not good enough and inadequate, easily intimidated, struggling to express my ideas and suggestions clearly, extreme difficulty in making decisions, and an inability to lead effectively even though I possessed most of the skills necessary. Do any of these challenges resonate with you?

In the past, I was often intimidated. I desperately wanted to be confident and command respect.

Each one of us chooses confidence or timidity - I am certain if you are reading this, you have excellent skills, ideas and thoughts; yet without the confidence to believe in your abilities and trust your instincts, your skills are wasted.

There are three steps I ultimately chose to take to strengthen my confidence:

◆ **Acknowledgement**: I recognized and admitted my lack of confidence;

◆ **Decision**–I made a conscious decision to build my confidence and believe in myself;

◆ **Commitment**–I committed to taking the necessary steps to create change, despite initial challenges.

Women's Worth and Impact Benefit the World

In any culture, women who are more confident contribute to a myriad of benefits for themselves and their society. It is important that women recognize and understand their worth, their impact, and their ability to contribute to the well-being of every person in that society.

To begin with, confident women are more likely to take good care of themselves physically, mentally, emotionally and spiritually. This leads to more harmonious family life, healthier children, and stronger communities. Confidence empowers women to pursue goals, insist on equal treatment and understand their rights in the workplace. Education improves, workplace atmosphere improves, leadership is more accountable, and the community at large is more successful and growth oriented. Confident women obtain higher-level positions, negotiate better salaries, and start their own businesses. This not only benefits them personally but also contributes to the broader economy by increasing productivity and innovation.

Confident women serve as role models helping to ensure future generations to believe in themselves and strive for their goals. This initiates a positive cycle of empowerment and aspiration. Confidence allows women to build strong, positive relationships, both personally and professionally; they are better equipped to communicate effectively, set boundaries, and advocate for themselves and others.

When women are confident and actively participate in all areas of society, making decisions is a more balanced, inclusive process, equitable solutions are achieved, creative problem solving serves the public good, and literally all of society benefits from women who are more confident and believe in themselves.

Yet, the issue of women's confidence continues to be ignored.

Although confident, powerful women are a necessary part of a flourishing society, the issue of women's confidence is not being solved. In some countries, women are still stoned to death. Malala Yousafzai was shot in the head simply because she wanted to attend school. And in the US, according to an article by Caitlynn Peetz (November 09, 2023) in EDUCATION WEEK "a major drop in girls' self-confidence between 2017... and 2023...." has occurred. According to the BBC World News (https://www.bbc.com/news/world-us-canada-53521143) in our Capitol Building amongst lawmakers, those who are supposed to embody decency, women are called "bitch" if they dare oppose the status quo.

Is there any hope for the future of our upcoming generations of young women? Indeed, there is! Through the voices of women such as the producers and writers of this book, the leadership of vibrant female role models like Malala Yousafzai, Jane Goodall, Oprah Winfrey, J.K. Rowling, and Serena Williams who were repressed and experienced failure before they succeeded, women see that strength, character, and confidence are vital for success and abundance. And, importantly, all are possible.

We must become all we can be so that the next generation has tools to make life better for everyone. The world, our communities, schools, the workplace, need changing - is it solely up to us individually? No! It takes all of us to help girls become strong women. First, we must empower ourselves, then we can empower others, together.

The virtuous cycle

The idea that confident, empowered women working together will make all women stronger is evidenced in several well-documented social, psychological, and economic principles (Empowerment of Women. https://www.unwomen.org/en/how-we-work/commission-on-the-status-of-women).

Confident women choose to work together and create strong support networks, providing emotional support, career advice, and networking opportunities. Women who have access to such networks advance further in careers, earn more money and are empowered.

Confident women become mentors, evidenced by my own experience and the experience of my colleagues. Women with less experience benefit; the benefits increase exponentially.

Confident women advocate more effectively for policies and practices that support gender equality. Collective voices have more influence, making it possible to initiate changes such as equal pay, maternity leave, and anti-discrimination policies.

Confidence increases collaboration among women and

brings diverse perspectives to the table, leading to more innovative solutions and better decision-making. Diversity in thought and experience enhances creativity and problem-solving in the workplace.

Confident, strong women support each other and create an environment of mutual empowerment. This builds further confidence and encourages women to pursue leadership roles, taking on challenges they might otherwise avoid. Women working together challenge harmful gender stereotypes by demonstrating competence, leadership, and collaboration, changing perception. Confidence and working together foster a sense of community and belonging, especially in fields, where women might otherwise feel isolated or marginalized.

The strength that comes from confidence, collaboration, and empowerment will change lives, communities, and education, improving life for everyone.

Your 30-Day Challenge

Days 1 - 7: journal, examine values and personal truth; culminating in an acknowledgement of necessity to change certain behaviors, habits, and self-talk. There will be a journal prompt every day designed to determine the most important values and to explore personal truth through personal experiences that lead to wisdom and, eventually, to sharing.

Days 8-14: decide whether change is necessary through positive self-talk, meditation, discussions, and support. If you're in a rut, feeling stuck, or struggling to make a decision as to what to do next, you'll find answers here. You'll have a guided meditation, journal prompts every day, and some ideas about positive self-talk and affirmations.

Days 15-22: develop a commitment to empowered confidence through story telling or writing, meditation, support, and group discussions. Using your preferred format: a video that tells a story or a written structure, you will be guided through telling your story. Another guided meditation will be available, group discussions, and guidance on how to share story.

Days 23-30: create a plan for the future with guidance and direction: knowing your values and truth will help you decide what you want your future to be. Through meditation, envisioning, story, discussion, and with guidance, you will develop steps to activate your plans for your future.

Take the next step by visiting my website! You'll find all the details on what to expect, the results you can achieve, and even a chance to schedule a free call to discuss your goals and ideas. I look forward to connecting with you! https://renaissanceedge.godaddysites.com/

About the Author

Susan Patterson brings a wealth of experience to the table. With ten years as a corporate legal assistant and another ten as an executive director in private associations, she ultimately found her passion in education. As a teacher, Susan has taught AP English, literature, writing, and English as a Second Language. She has also trained teachers in classroom management, effective teaching methods, and strategies for engaging both advanced and reluctant students.

Susan's teaching journey has taken her to the US, Mexico, and Egypt. She holds certifications as both an International Baccalaureate and Advanced Placement Educator. Her PhD dissertation examined the similarities and differences among developed and developing nations in order to pinpoint effective strategies directly applicable to education systems and the classroom.

Susan now guides women to find their true voice and grow into their power. She created the CLEARE program (Six Steps to Change Everything), teaches workshops, leads groups, and offers eBooks and workbooks to provide guided self-study.

Susan is a six-time bestselling author. She has published articles, curricula, poetry, non-fiction, self-study workbooks, eBooks and two novels. Guiding others and sharing wisdom is part of Susan's perspective, mission, and purpose.

M. S. Patterson
Renaissance Edge
edge.patt@gmail.com
https://www.linkedin.com/in/m-susan-patterson-69a507185/

STACEY HALL

Dedication

To everyone who desires to harness their own power to achieve their goals!

CHAPTER 10

HOW TO HARNESS YOUR POWER AND ACHIEVE YOUR GOALS

By Stacey Hall

The Path of Self-Alignment.

The Universal Law of Vibration reminds us of the immense power we hold to improve our reality by staying on that path through self-alignment. By understanding and harmonizing the principles of energy, vibration, and resonance, we can transcend our current circumstances to actively – and finally – create the life we desire.

Consider how adjusting the sails of a boat can help it navigate more efficiently, ensuring it moves smoothly and maintains its course despite varying wind conditions. Similarly, vibrational alignment works in much the same way; the direction a person's life takes is influenced by their emotional state or vibrational frequency, steering them toward their desired outcomes.

Living in fear, anger, and guilt can significantly diminish a person's overall quality of life by affecting their mental, emotional, and physical well-being. These low-vibration emotions can prevent individuals from enjoying their lives, achieving their goals, and forming meaningful connections with others due to anxiety, emotional instability, relationship conflicts, physical health issues, sleep disorders, negative thinking patterns, problems in the workplace, and impaired decision-making.

Conversely, positive emotions, like joy, love, and gratitude, are associated with higher frequencies, which produce constructive mindsets enhancing our overall well-being and effectiveness.

Manifesting our Deepest Desires is within our Power.

To manifest our deepest desires and values, we must align with their vibrational frequencies. This concept is based on the idea that everything in the universe, including our thoughts and emotions, operates on specific frequencies. When our internal state matches the frequency of our desired reality, we become powerful co-creators of our lives.

However, when we are out of alignment—when our thoughts, emotions, and actions contradict our true desires and values— we disrupt the natural flow of energy. This misalignment can lead to frustration, confusion, and a sense of being "stuck." These negative experiences indicate a need to recalibrate our inner state to restore harmony.

Just as a guitar must be tuned to the correct pitch to play harmoniously, our inner state must resonate with our goals. Operating from a place of clarity, intention, and positivity, we send out vibrations that attract the reality we want to manifest.

Achieving this alignment requires deliberate and empowered steps toward our goals, along with an unwavering belief in our ability to achieve them. This belief transforms abstract desires into tangible outcomes. By maintaining a clear vision and taking consistent, positive actions, we harmonize our internal frequencies with our external aspirations.

In this state of alignment, we are guided by an inner certainty that our desires are possible and inevitable. Through self-alignment, we unlock the potential to create a life that reflects our highest aspirations and values.

Science is beginning to Explore this Energy.

Robert Puff Ph.D. host and producer of The Happiness Podcast, with 16+ million downloads, writes in Psychology Today, "alignment starts and ends with listening to our hearts and bodies. When we look inward, we can gather so much vital information about ourselves and what fulfills us and what doesn't.

Then we can use that information and steer our energy towards the things that bring us peace and happiness."*

Susan Simpson is Director of Coach Training at PAIRIN, with the mission to see the potential in every person and uncover the value they bring to an organization. Based on research, she wrote "people high in Self-Alignment sense a minimal discrepancy between their actual self and the type of person they would like to be. When this sense of congruence is rooted in genuine self-worth, they feel little need to defend or boast. Poised and self-accepting, they are quick to value and extend high regard to others." Healthy individuals recognize that Self-Alignment is an ongoing process. As they develop, people become more informed, both as to how they are and how they would ideally like to be. As with all building processes, there will be reality checks, miscalculations and construction redos along the way. And as with all building plans, the ideal self is

not static and will typically have many revisions."
*https://www.psychologytoday.com/us/blog/meditation-modern-life/202108/how-become-aligned-life
https://www.pairin.com/self-alignment-becoming-dream-home/

How Research Support Embracing this Mindset

According to Carl Rogers and supported by PAIRIN's research, "Healthy individuals recognize that Self-Alignment is an ongoing process. As they develop, people become more informed, both as to how they are and how they would ideally like to be. And as with all building plans, the ideal self is not static and will typically have many revisions."

Gary Latham, an award-winning researcher, author, and professor of organizational effectiveness at Rotman, has studied goal setting and performance. Based on his research shared in a 2002 retrospective he co-wrote in American Psychologist, titled 'Building a Practically Useful Theory of Goal Setting and Task Motivation,' "when self-set goals are aligned with assigned goals, individual performance improves."

In 2011, I wrote the #1 global best-seller, '*Chi-To-Be! Achieving Your Ultimate B-All*,' in which I shared 12 ways to raise your vibration to achieve your goals. I received thousands of testimonials for this process, including "Stacey, if I could climb through my computer to give you a BIG HUG, I would do it right now!!! Tonight, I started reading your book. Those 5 steps you provided to raise our vibration were AMAZING!!! I was in tears because they helped with my decision over the battle that I've been fighting with myself lately!! I now see things more clearly, and I am so grateful!! THANK YOU!!!!" https://www-2.rotman.utoronto.ca/insightshub/leadership-career-development/goal-alignment https://www.amazon.com/Chi-Be-Stacey-Hall-ebook/dp/B005CXO6KK/

Your 30-Day Challenge

Based on my vibration-boosting, goal-achieving Chi-To-Be! Process, here are the 5 steps I suggest to harness your power and align with your deepest desires and values to achieve any goal:

1. Cultivate Self-Awareness: From Day 1 - 6, schedule time to identify your true desires, values, and beliefs by making a list of all of them. Then, put them in priority order. Each day, start and end your day looking at your list.

2. Practice Mindfulness: From Day 7 - 12, continue to cultivate self-awareness by implementing mindfulness as you take actions aligned with your desires, values, and beliefs. Mindfulness helps you recognize what causes you to feel frustration, confusion, overwhelm, or being stuck so you can make other choices or change your perspective.

3. Follow Your Intuition: From Day 13 - 18, continue to cultivate self-awareness and practice mindfulness while keeping a journal to record the moments you feel you are guided by your intuition towards making choices and taking action - rather than following someone else's advice or what your mind thinks you 'should' do.

4. Notice Resistance: From Day 19 - 24, continue to cultivate self-awareness, practice mindfulness, and follow your intuition. Keep a 2nd journal to record the moments you still feel resistance and frustration and why (fear of failure, fear of change, self-doubt, etc.)

5. Reframe Your Thoughts: From Day 25 - 30, continue to cultivate self-awareness, practice mindfulness, follow your intuition, and reframe negative thoughts. For example, instead of thinking, "I can't do this," reframe to "I am capable of overcoming challenges."

During this 30-Day Exploration also be mindful of your nutrition, hydration, movement, and experience complementary modalities, such as acupuncture, energy healing, and sound therapy to raise your vibration and align your body's energy system to achieve success.

Resources:
https://onlinelibrary.wiley.com/doi/full/10.1002/mba2.71#:~:text=According%20to%20quantum%20theory%2C%20matter,be%20the%20medicine%20of%20frequencies.
https://drkezchirolab.com/blogs/news/the-power-of-vibrational-frequency-and-your-emotional-guidancesystem#:~:text=Your%20current%20emotional%20state%20falls,misalignment%20with%20your%20inner%20being.
https://www.bridgestonetire.com/learn/maintenance/tire-alignment/#

What stops you from making sales? Do you secretly feel that making offers is pushy and spammy? Are you unsure how and when to make an offer? You are not alone. It's a common challenge that many entrepreneurs face - the disheartening feeling of not knowing how to start conversations and engage in a way that is captivating to your audience, so they want to say YES to your offers. This lack of success is confidence-draining and can leave you wondering, "How will I ever achieve my sales goals?" Are you now ready to transform this frustration into your sales success?

Watch this 2-Part Webinar now and discover the key that unlocks the secret to making effortless sales.

https://www.sellingfromyourcomfortzone.com/simple-sales-success

About the Author

In 2004, Stacey Hall physically, emotionally, and mentally ran out of energy and enthusiasm to take her accomplishments to the next level of success. She began a journey of aligning her physical, emotional, and mental energy at a consistently high vibration in order to achieve all of her goals.

She wrote 'Chi-To-Be! Achieving Your Ultimate B-All' to share the essential tools, resources, and support which harmonized her body, mind, emotions and spirit so that others can achieve a level of well-being they may not know exists.

Since then, she has taken 5 books to global #1 best-seller status. She is known for her TEDx Talk on 'How to Stop Should-ing on Yourself' and her myth-busting sales strategy program. 'Selling From Your Comfort Zone," which has helped thousands of business owners and sales professionals create more sales, satisfaction, and success.

As Stacey explains, the comfort zone is your power zone. Shifting away from pushy sales tactics, she will show how you can bring meaning to how you serve others through your business. You will discover a simple formula for a personalized approach to connection-building through problem-solving by remaining in alignment with your calling, with yourself, and with what you are selling.

Stacey Hall
Success with Stacey Hall
goforyeswithstaceyhall@gmail.com
https://www.linkedin.com/in/staceyhall1/

"Each time a woman stands up for herself, without knowing it possibly, without claiming it, she stands up for all women."

— Maya Angelou

Part 3: Wellness

LORALEE HUMPHERYS

Dedication

Dedicated to the women of this planet. May they again cherish, honor and love their bodies and themselves. May they come again to the recognition of the Divine Feminine as she expresses herself through the nuances of grace and form of their beautiful bodies. May women learn to confidently reclaim their creative power, and boldly speak their truths, standing in the authority of their Authentic Sovereign BEingness.

CHAPTER 11

ELEVATE YOUR LIFE: 30 DAYS TO PAIN-FREE DIGESTION

By Loralee Humpherys

The Big Picture of Digestive Issues

While many approaches to solving digestive issues offer relief, I find many important pieces are missing. Some produce only short-term relief, covering up symptoms with medication. Others offer solutions with dietary changes and supplements, yet they don't get to the root cause. After several months the problems start presenting again.

Identifying the root cause of digestive issues and resolving them is my focus. Only then can true, permanent healing occur. To do that, we look to natural healing principles that have been successfully used for hundreds of years. One reason why digestive issues are so rampant today is because people have turned away from - or have never been taught - natural health and healing.

The approach to lasting gut health is to understand and consistently apply these holistic approaches. . Not only are you addressing dietary changes, you're also revamping lifestyle habits, how you think about yourself and feel about your life.

Without seeing yourself through this multifaceted lens, it's easy to wander in circles, confused and exhausted as to why you can't seem to resolve your gut disturbances.

My 30-Day Guide sets you on the path to approach your digestive issues from a holistic perspective. Leading you step-by-step in a well thought out progression of activities, you can find relief without overwhelm.

Upon completion of it, you may be pleasantly surprised with how good you feel both physically and emotionally. And you'll discover the steps and information needed to finally put your digestive issues behind you. For Good!

The Politics of Information

The Flexner Report of 1910 brought extensive and devastating repercussions. This was used to give the budding pharmaceutical industry political influence to target schools and wellness centers of natural medicine. Lost revenues caused many to shut down. Holistic doctors in all disciplines were discredited, lost their licenses and thus their livelihoods.

This gave way to the monopoly and influence of big pharma and drug-based medicine. Today most people aren't taught how to care for their bodies. Prior to this, natural healing practices were common knowledge, without costly drugs and surgery.

A research company, Ipsos, did a poll in May 2023. It found that 1/3 of Americans regularly experience abdominal discomfort or pain, and 38% talk to their doctor about it. Yet 31% don't feel their doctor takes their concerns seriously.

Half of Americans would rather talk to a digestive health specialist. . Forty percent prefer talking to family/friends instead of their doctor and rely on the internet for gut health advice.

The poll asked participants' general knowledge about caring for the gut and what causes digestive issues. It reveals a considerable lack of understanding. These findings don't speak well for the traditional approach of doctor visits that women have turned to for solutions.

It is an alarming state of affairs that such a large portion of the population suffer with digestive issues because of how we eat and live, including the low nutritional quality of food and rampant contamination of harmful ingredients.

Many people's unhealthy habits and food choices are dictated by quick convenience; regardless of quality and the havoc it creates in the digestive system. When organs like brain, endocrine and nervous tissues don't receive the required nutrients to properly function, they inevitably break down.

When your digestion complains and causes pain, this is a loud message that changes need to be made.

Dietary, Lifestyle, and Medical Interventions

Many heed this message and search for solutions. Current recommendations to address digestive issues focus on dietary and lifestyle changes and sometimes medical interventions. Five common ones are:

1. **Dietary Changes.** High fiber, plant based whole foods

of herbs, fruits, vegetables, whole grains, legumes, nuts and seeds will calm and regulate digestion. Foodstuffs that are inflammatory, congestive, bio-engineered, refined and highly processed must be eliminated. Including allergy causing foods like dairy, soy and gluten. This often resolves many problems.

Adding probiotics through supplements or fermented foods like high quality yogurt, kefirs and sauerkraut support a healthy gut microbiome. Digestive enzymes can help break down food, reducing symptoms like gas and bloating.

2. **Drink Plenty of Pure Water**. Staying hydrated helps with digestion and the absorption of nutrients. It also helps prevent constipation. Drink at least 8 cups a day.

3. **Regular Exercise.** Physical activity like walking, running or strength training stimulates peristalsis, preventing issues like constipation and bloating.

4. **Reduce Stress.** High stress levels are a significant contributor to poor digestion. Mindfulness, meditation, energy work and emotional healing, journaling, deep breathing exercises, and yoga are effective stress management techniques.

5. **Supplements or Medical Interventions**. Popular over-the-counter aids like antacids, laxatives, and anti-diarrhea medications are often habit forming and only provide short term relief. Herbal teas, essential oils and nutrient supplementation are natural remedies that have no adverse side effects.

For persistent digestive issues, a healthcare provider can

recommend specific treatments and dietary adjustments based on individual needs. These often include drugs, which cause additional issues from side effects.

Evidence of the Effect of New Diet and Lifestyle Habits

The challenge in correcting digestive issues is forming new diet and lifestyle habits. This is the work of healing yourself. My Radiant Reset Program is tailored to assist you in doing this and teaches you to view your health through a holistic lens. You learn to restore your digestion by applying methods of natural healing instead of drugs.

These individuals and I did just that. They're either clients or associates I have known. If we did it, you can too!

Years of poor diet and antibiotics left Michael in pain with eczema, Candida overgrowth, bloating, brain fog, fatigue and poor sleep. Low self-esteem, depression and anxiety fostered drugs and partying.

He learned to cleanse his body and digestive organs and adopted a plant-based diet. Becoming more mindful, he formed new habits of speaking to himself in a loving, accepting way instead of in a critical, self-sabotaging way. His digestive issues, pain, Candida and skin cleared up, eyes brightened, and sleep improved. He released unhealthy relationships and became happy, energized, motivated and focused.

For years I was depressed, pessimistic, angry and dissatisfied with work. I ate this away with cravings and emotional eating, eventually suffering with gut irritation, pain, bloating and excess weight. I learned to respect and appreciate my body. Caring for it became an interest and priority. I changed to a plant-based diet and engaged in emotional healing work. Cravings and digestive issues disappeared, and comfort foods lost their appeal. I dropped 20 pounds, and am optimistic, happy, confident, focused and enjoy working.

Childhood chronic constipation and painful elimination left Camille thin, malnourished, bloated, with poor memory, skin issues, cravings, high stress and anxiety. She started walking regularly, changed her diet, and cleansed the buildup of waste from her intestines. She learned to manage stress better and adopted a more positive, self-loving mindset, her bowel became regular and painless, weight normalized, skin and mind cleared. Confident in how to care for herself, she became happy, energized and off all medication.

Your 30-Day Challenge
Consistent application of these foundational steps from my Radiant Reset Program can offer profound effects on your digestion!

Week One: Lower Inflammation by eating plant-based foods daily - fruits, vegetables, herbs, nuts, seeds, legumes. Examples:
Green smoothies: spinach, kale, banana, berries, cherries, flax and chia seeds, high quality protein powder with pea, hemp proteins, grasses powders.

Salads: carrots, broccoli, cucumber, bell peppers, quinoa, legumes, kale, spinach, nuts, olives, avocado, sunflower seeds, apples, grapes, fresh lemon juice, coconut oil, balsamic vinegar.

Week Two: Calm your nervous system through this breathing exercise. Breathe in for 7 counts, hold 3 counts, exhale 7 counts, hold 3 counts. Repeat 3-5 minutes as needed, until you feel calm.

Daily drink herbal teas:

◆ Schizandra, Reishi, Lions Mane mushrooms to support brain and nerve health.

◆ Chamomile or Valerian to lower anxiety and improve sleep.

◆ GABA - to calm the brain.

Week Three: Journal to pay attention to the mental chatter and any resistance to changing your diet and to identify any unresolved emotions perpetuating your gut issues. Write down things during your day that trigger you. Identify repeating patterns that throw you off center. Awareness is the first step to resolve sugar cravings and emotional eating!

Week Four: Exercise and Movement. Walk outside each morning for 30 minutes to stimulate lymph and intestinal peristalsis. Walk barefoot on the grass for 15 minutes. This grounds you and clears chaotic EMF energies from your body that agitate your nervous system and increase cortisol, the stress and belly fat hormone.

Are you ready to take the next step in healing your digestion naturally? Get my free gift that explains the root cause of digestive issues and introduces you to the next critical phase of restoring your gut health - cleansing.

Download my Free Guide, "The Secret No One's Told You About to Finally Free Yourself Of Pesky Painful Gut Issues ...For Good!" Discover the root cause underlying your digestive issues, and the often overlooked solution. Learn tried and true methods to take back control of your digestive health, your body and your life! Get it here: https://loralee-humpherys.aweb.page/p/152330d5-d010-4280-a2bb-e55ee0ef92e0

About the Author

Loralee Humpherys, the creator of the Radiant Reset Program, inspires spiritual, professional, stressed-out women to break free of deep-seated social conditioning and beliefs that keep them feeling stuck, fearful and in poor digestive health. And instead, know that you can heal yourself through living in harmony with Natural Laws of Health and being in alignment with your authentic self.

For years Loralee struggled with emotional eating and digestive upsets, driven in part by her quest to make peace with herself, her body and her life. Wanting freedom from them, her research led her to discover principles of natural healing, cleansing and detoxification, energy healing and holistic nutrition.

Loralee is a Spiritual Health Coach, Massage Therapist and Reiki Master, with experience in Meditation and Aromatherapy. From this extensive experience, she developed the skill of sensing energies held within client's bodies and to assist them in releasing stagnant ones. This and many other experiences brought her to an understanding of the intimate connection between physical health, mental and emotional well-being.

Loralee Humpherys
Nourishing Essentials Lifestyle Consulting
Loralee@nourishing-essentials.com
https://www.linkedin.com/in/loralee-humpherys-4959b62b3/

"Her own thoughts and reflections were habitually her best companions."
— **Jane Austen**

CHERI PETRONI

Dedication

To my husband, Ron, who's been my partner in overcoming obstacles and building a prosperous life together for over 40 years.

CHAPTER 12

HARMONIZE YOUR BODY'S ENERGIES TO BOOST WEALTH

By Cheri Petroni

For everyone ready to boost their wealth!

Let's face it, we all have moments when we are not 100%. Times when we don't feel vibrant and abundant. This is an energy imbalance. Our energy is composed of physical, emotional, mental, and spiritual energy centers. When they aren't working in unison, our energies are in disharmony.

Think of these energy centers as parts of a car. When a car gets a tune-up, it runs smoothly.

Similarly, when harmonized centers are "tuned up", they amplify motivation, fuel passion, and drive actions that create wealth. Energy bodies in balance lead to greater success.

When your energy centers are unbalanced, it can really affect your income potential!

Unbalanced energies often lead to chronic stress, mental fog, and emotional ups and downs, which can undermine your productivity and decision-making. You might find yourself working harder without seeing financial rewards, as scattered energy makes it tough to focus and seize opportunities.

Plus, misalignment can keep you stuck with limiting beliefs about money and success. These are often rooted in past experiences, generational beliefs, and traumas. Clearing these roadblocks and shifting beliefs can open up new financial abundance.

When you clear mental and emotional barriers, you start to see opportunities you might have missed before. Your renewed energy and positive mindset can lead to better decisions and actions that naturally increase your income, helping you create the prosperous life you deserve.

It is paramount that your energy is balanced. This harmony is the first step in bringing clarity, boosting confidence, and creating a magnetic presence that attracts wealth and prosperity into your life.

Many of us are unaware of our energetic presence. We run on autopilot, ignoring challenges and roadblocks, and pushing them aside, while working longer hours and stressing over small details. Juggling careers, family, and personal goals often leaves us feeling stretched thin and unfulfilled, which can take a toll on our motivation, energy, and vitality.

Our four energy centers work together to harmonize our energy field. When one body is out of balance, the others work harder to balance the field, creating an energy field that is in disharmony. This disharmony is akin to driving a car with one flat tire—progress is slow, and the ride is bumpy.

Signs of "Flat Tire" Energy:
1. **Financial Instability:** Constant worry about making ends meet that leads to chronic stress and worry
2. **Constant Anxiety:** Anxiousness drains energy, leaving

you too exhausted to seize new opportunities.
3. **Poor Decision-Making:** Inability to focus and think clearly results in missed opportunities and regret.
4. **Feeling Stuck:** Paralyzed and unable to advance in your career or personal goals, leading to frustration and dissatisfaction.
5. **Scarcity Mindset:** Believing there's never enough, which perpetuates feelings of lack and prevents financial growth.

Signs of Harmonized Energy:
1. **Attracting Financial Success:** Naturally draws in opportunities for wealth, leading to increased financial stability and peace of mind.
2. **Making Better Financial Decisions:** Clarity and focus help you make smart choices, resulting in more effective use of resources and long-term financial growth.
3. **Seizing Growth Opportunities:** With balanced energy, you are more alert and ready to take advantage of opportunities that propel your career and personal life forward.
4. **Developing a Prosperity Mindset:** Embracing abundance and positivity allows you to break free from limiting beliefs and embracing infinite possibilities for wealth creation.
5. **Enhanced Creativity and Innovation:** Harmony aligns with creative thinking, allowing you to find innovative solutions and pursue exciting new ventures with enthusiasm.

Fresh, harmonized energy transforms your financial reality. It allows you to create a more fulfilling and prosperous life, where you're not simply surviving, but truly thriving.

"The ability of the brain to change — to adapt based on the environment, stimuli or experiences — is termed broadly as neuroplasticity," says Mayo Clinic expert Prashanthi Vemuri, Ph.D., who researches the brain and neurodegenerative disorders (Mayo Clinic)

Several studies support the idea that aligning values and actions, while rewiring the brain, can increase income potential. Neuroplasticity is the brain's ability to reorganize itself by forming new neural connections and plays a crucial role in how we can change our thinking patterns and behaviors. A study highlighted by Psychology Today shows that neuroplasticity can help individuals overcome negative thinking and misaligned energy, leading to a more positive and resilient mindset, which is essential for financial success (Psychology Today).

Furthermore, research from Harvard University found that early life experiences, including those related to financial stress and parental education, significantly shape brain development and cognitive functions, which are critical for making informed financial decisions and recognizing opportunities (Harvard DASH).
https://mcpress.mayoclinic.org/healthy-aging/the-power-of-neuroplasticity-how-your-brain-adapts-and-grows-as-you-age/
https://www.psychologytoday.com/us/blog/making-the-whole-beautiful/202404/rewiring-the-traumatized-brain-for-positivity
https://dash.harvard.edu/bitstream/handle/1/23845261/4414816.pdf?sequence=1#:~:text=

Dr. Jacob Towery MD, Adjunct Clinical Faculty at Stanford University School of Medicine shares, "While mindsets can be helpful for distilling information and managing expectations, they can also be maladaptive, leading to interpersonal problems and feelings of guilt, inadequacy, sadness and anxiety."

He also shares, "the good news is mindsets are highly changeable, and if you are willing to learn the technology of changing your mindset and defeating your distorted thoughts, you can have significantly more happiness." (Stanford News)

This leads me to Debbie, a client who struggled with making ends meet. Despite making good money and working with a financial counselor, she wasn't making headway. In our first conversation, it became clear that Debbie's childhood trauma had left her with a deep sense of unworthiness, which she tried to soothe through a shopping addiction.

We started by addressing her feelings of unworthiness, uncovering an intricate web of beliefs that didn't serve her. Through our work, Debbie became aware of how her physical, emotional, mental, and spiritual energies were in disharmony, impacting her financial stability.

As we focused on balancing her energies and creating a new web of beliefs, Debbie began tapping into her mental clarity and spiritual abundance, empowering her financial decisions. She learned to choose long-term security over the instant gratification of shopping. Each day, she grows stronger, with a notable increase in financial abundance and the power to make thoughtful choices. https://news.stanford.edu/stories/2021/09/mindsets-clearing-lens-life

Debbie's transformation shows the power of awareness, alignment, and updating one's mindset to one of possibility and hope. It's my pleasure to offer you a taste of her journey and how it can inspire your own path to financial and personal success.

30 Days to Harmony Challenge
1. Choose any one of the Daily Activities
2. Spend 5-10 minutes with the Activity
3. Reflect and journal for 5-10 minutes

Daily Activities

◆ **Guided Visualization:** Get comfortable. Close your eyes. Imagine a peaceful, safe place. Visualize the sights, sounds, and smells.

◆ **Breath Awareness:** Close your eyes. Focus on your breath. Notice the air moving in and out; as air enters your nostrils, your lungs, and as you exhale.

◆ **Walking in Nature:** Walk slowly and quietly feel the ground. Observe surrounding sounds, sights, smells, and sensations.

◆ **Listening to High-Vibration Music:** Get comfortable. Listen to music or nature sounds. Focus on any shifts within you.

◆ **Toning the Body:** Relax. Take a deep breath. Exhale loudly. Feel your body's vibration. Notice how it shifts, moving from the toes to the head

Reflect and Journal, including expressions of gratitude.

◆ What thoughts and feelings come up?

◆ What patterns or behaviors show up?

◆ How do they relate to you?

◆ What are you grateful for?

The insights you gain from daily practice will lay a foundation for transformation. The next step is to download "Your Earliest Money Story" Guided Meditation, my gift to you. This Guided Meditation will expand your new-found knowledge and continue to support you in harmonizing your energies to make empowering financial decisions and to increase your income potential.

"Your Earliest Money Story" Guided Meditation to transform your financial well-being and experience abundant living. https://www.cheripetroni.com/special

About the Author

Cheri Petroni is a leading expert in aligning and harmonizing the physical, emotional, mental, and spiritual bodies to achieve holistic success. She is dedicated to helping women overcome pain in health, wealth, and relationships by addressing inner child trauma and clearing roadblocks to success. In 2014, Cheri founded Oasis to Zen Transformation Spa in Las Vegas, Nevada, "Where inner and outer beauty become wellness."

Cheri holds a master's degree in education, specializing in early childhood education and development from the University of Nevada Las Vegas. She has extensive certifications and years of training as a trauma-informed success coach, with Margaret Lynch Raniere, as well as Lion Goodman, founder of The Clear Beliefs Institute, where she supports mentor coaches in training. Cheri also studies with Eric Edmeades as a Certified WILDFIT™ Wellness Coach and holds certification in Nutrition Microscopy.

Her wellness journey began in the spa industry, expanding to online transformational work in 2016. Her teaching experience helped her identify and heal childhood trauma's lingering effects in adults, enabling clients to achieve success in all life areas. Cheri's mission is to support business professionals held back by trauma, guiding them to live lives of fulfillment and joy through self-discovery and growth.

Cheri Petroni
Trauma-informed Transformation Coach
cheri@cheripetroni.com
https://www.linkedin.com/in/cheripetroni/

MONIKA GRECZEK

Dedication

To everyone whose hair matters to your well-being, self-esteem and confidence.

CHAPTER 13

GORGEOUS AND HEALTHY HAIR IN 30 DAYS!

By Monika Greczek

The reason it is so important to have an optimal hair and scalp health plan is several problems can arise when we don't, like these:

1. **Scalp Issues:** Without proper care, the scalp can become oily or dry, leading to dandruff, itchiness, and irritation. This can also cause inflammation and infections if not addressed.

2. **Hair Damage:** Improper care can result in hair becoming brittle, weak, and prone to breakage. Over time, this can lead to split ends and significant hair loss, reducing overall hair volume and health.

3. **Product Buildup:** Using the wrong products or not properly cleansing the scalp can lead to a buildup of styling products, oils, and dirt. This can clog hair follicles, inhibit healthy hair growth, and cause scalp discomfort.

4. **Nutrient Deficiency:** Without nourishing treatments, the scalp may lack essential nutrients, which can affect the health and vitality of the hair. This can result in dull, lifeless hair and hinder natural growth.

5. **Lack of Strength:** Neglecting strengthening treatments can make hair more susceptible to environmental damage, mechanical stress from styling, and chemical treatments. This can lead to weakened hair structure and increased shedding.

6. **Poor Maintenance:** Failing to maintain and protect scalp health can result in long-term issues such as chronic dryness, sensitivity to environmental factors, and a persistent unhealthy scalp condition. This can also affect the overall appearance and manageability of hair.

Overall, a lack of a proper hair and scalp health plan can lead to persistent and worsening hair and scalp issues, reducing the quality, appearance, and health of your hair.

To ensure these problems are fixed or do not occur in the first place, let's begin with addressing hair damage and preventing breakage. Healthy hair is less prone to split ends and brittleness, which allows it to grow longer and look more vibrant. Proper hair care routines, including the right shampoos, conditioners, and treatments, help preserve hair's natural oils and moisture, ensuring it remains resilient against environmental stressors and styling damage.

Clearing product buildup is just as important. A clean scalp without excess oil and residue can breathe better, allowing hair follicles to function optimally. This promotes healthier hair growth and reduces the risk of clogged follicles, which can lead to thinning hair and scalp discomfort.

Nourishing hair with deep conditioning treatments and scalp scrubs are vital for hair health. These treatments strengthen hair from the roots, enhancing its overall vitality and luster. Protein treatments fortify hair, making it less susceptible to breakage and environmental damage.

Finally, maintaining and protecting scalp health ensures long-term benefits. Regular care, including essential oil massages and leave-in conditioners, shields the scalp and hair from external stressors, while a balanced diet and proper hydration support overall scalp and hair wellness. Solving these issues not only improves the appearance and health of your hair but also boosts self-confidence and overall well-being.

Achieving optimal scalp health is currently tackled through scientific research, consumer demand for clean beauty products,& awareness of scalp care's significance for overall hair health.

Scientific Research: It has been seen that modern day styling methods and use of different hair care products have resulted in hair loss and also cause hair damage. The process of chipping of the hair cuticle, which results from abrasion of hair due to grooming devices or chemicals, is a major factor in hair damage. Hair texture is related to the scalp condition.

Clean Beauty Movement: A surge in demand for clean beauty products, including those for hair and scalp care. Consumers increasingly scrutinize product ingredients, seeking formulations free of sulfates, parabens, and other harmful chemicals. Brands respond by creating hair care products with natural, plant-based ingredients renowned for their nourishing and gentle properties.

Education & Awareness: Efforts are underway to educate consumers about scalp health's importance and its impact on hair quality. Beauty influencers, dermatologists,& hair care experts share tips, routines, & product recommendations to help individuals maintain a healthy scalp. Social media and online forums serve as platforms for discussions and information sharing on scalp care.

Clinical Trials and Product Development: Beauty companies conduct clinical trials to assess their scalp care products' efficacy and safety. These trials yield crucial data on ingredient performance, guiding product development and marketing strategies.

The good news is that achieving optimal scalp health is being studied and advanced through ongoing scientific research, consumer education, and the creation of innovative clean beauty products for maintaining resilient, beautiful hair.

The daily administration of a proprietary nutritional supplement significantly increased hair growth after 90 and 180 days. This was evidenced by quantitative measurements and subjective self-assessments from the study participants. The initial findings after 90 days demonstrated noticeable hair growth, which was further amplified after an additional 90 days of treatment. This progressive improvement over 180 days indicates that the supplement's effects not only persist but may even enhance with prolonged use, suggesting that continuous administration could lead to sustained benefits in hair growth.

Moreover, the self-perceived improvements reported by participants after the initial 90 days were even more pronounced after 180 days of continued treatment. This suggests a cumulative effect, where the longer the supplement was taken, the more significant the perceived improvements in hair volume, density, and overall health. Such self-assessment data underscore the potential long-term benefits of the supplement from the user's perspective, highlighting its effectiveness over an extended period.

Importantly, no adverse events were reported throughout the study, indicating that the supplement is safe for daily use. The absence of negative side effects adds a layer of confidence in recommending this supplement for long-term use.

Your 30-Day Challenge

I invite you to implement this 30-Day Hair and Scalp Care Plan to transform and strengthen your scalp and hair.

Day 1-7: Detoxify and Cleanse. Start by detoxifying your scalp with a scalp and hair shampoo and sulfate-free clarifying shampoo. This removes impurities and product buildup, laying the groundwork for healthier hair.

Day 8-14: Nourish and Hydrate. Nourish your scalp with nutrient-rich ingredients like avocado, coconut oil, and argan oil. Treat yourself to deep conditioning treatments and exfoliate with a scalp scrub to replenish moisture and promote scalp health.

Day 15-21: Strengthen and Protect. Strengthen your hair follicles with protein treatments using ingredients like egg and yogurt. Protect your scalp from environmental stressors with essential oil massages and leave-in conditioners.

Day 22-30: Maintain and Sustain. Continue to support your scalp health with daily hydration, balanced nutrition, and gentle hair care routines. Use this time to reinforce the habits you've developed throughout the challenge for long-term scalp vitality.

Throughout the challenge, observe changes in your scalp condition and hair appearance. Look out for reduced dandruff, decreased itchiness, improved hair texture, and enhanced overall scalp health. Share your progress and experiences with others participating in the challenge to stay motivated and inspired.

By the end of the 30 days, you'll not only have achieved optimal scalp health but also developed sustainable habits for maintaining beautiful, resilient hair. Let's embark on this journey together and unlock the potential of your scalp and hair with clean, natural ingredients!

Win a Virtual Spa Hair & Scalp Detox Consultation – enter here: https://powerfulwomentoday.myflodesk.com/

About the Author

Monika Greczek is a noted professional in the hair industry as a Holistic Hair Coach, Owner of Extasy Hair Studio and Spa, Natura Hemp Co., and The Virtual Spa! She has been highlighted by P.O.W.E.R. (Professional Organization of Women Excellence Recognized).

She has studied, trained, and continued her education for

over 30 years. Her specialty is understanding the harmful toxins so prevalent in the industry and how to detoxify them. Her process incorporates sustainable habits for maintaining beautiful, resilient hair. Monika expanded her salon and spa to provide services, such as organic facials, massages using essential oils, and products that are para-bin, sulfate free, and better for us, using the most natural ingredients. Monika invites us all to unlock the potential of our scalp and hair with clean, natural ingredients!

Monika Greczek
The Virtual Spa
mgreczek16@gmail.com
https://www.linkedin.com/in/monika-greczek-3710b225/

"Women have always been the strong ones of the world."
— Coco Chanel

Part 4: Relationships

DONNA BARRON

Dedication
To my Fiancé Brian Francis Patella

CHAPTER 14

BECOMING IRRESISTIBLE: HOW TO ATTRACT YOUR IDEAL PARTNER

By Donna Barron

Becoming Irresistible

Many women struggle with understanding what it takes to attract and sustain a fulfilling relationship, often repeating negative patterns and carrying baggage from past experiences. This cycle can lead to frustration and disappointment, hindering the ability to form healthy, lasting connections. The root of this problem often lies in unresolved emotional issues and a lack of self-awareness. Without addressing these underlying factors, it's easy to fall into the same dysfunctional dynamics.

Emotional baggage from past relationships can get in the way of understanding and appreciating men, cloud judgment and impact self-esteem, and lead to making poor choices in partners, such as choosing partners who are emotionally unavailable or engaging in self-sabotaging behaviors.

These issues can create additional problems. For one, low self-esteem and emotional baggage can lead to a lack of trust, both in yourself and in others. This can cause anxiety and insecurity, making it difficult to form deep, meaningful connections. And, these negative patterns can erode your sense of self-worth, leading you to settle for less than you deserve in relationships.

Plus, these struggles can affect other areas of life. Chronic relationship stress can spill over into your professional life. It can also strain friendships and family relationships, as the emotional toll of repeated relationship failures can lead to withdrawal and isolation.

Without addressing these core issues, the cycle continues, making it increasingly difficult to find and maintain a fulfilling relationship.

All about Emotional Baggage

By letting go of this emotional baggage, you free yourself from the past and open up to new, healthier possibilities. When you know what you want and need in a relationship, you can set boundaries and make decisions that align with your well-being. This clarity fosters mutual respect and understanding, forming a solid foundation for a healthy, fulfilling relationship. Ultimately, this process empowers you to break free from negative patterns and create a love life that is both positive and sustainable.

When we are in a loving, supportive partnership, it significantly enhances our overall well-being, providing emotional stability, companionship, and a sense of purpose. Conversely, being in an unhealthy or unfulfilling relationship can lead to emotional distress, decreased self-esteem, and even physical health issues.

It is essential for women to learn to articulate their values and needs, set healthy boundaries, and communicate effectively, which are crucial skills for maintaining a long-lasting relationship. This transformation not only attracts the right partner, but also fosters a sense of inner confidence and clarity

Healthy relationships contribute to personal growth, mutual respect, and a harmonious living environment. They serve as a foundation for building families, achieving personal goals, and creating a supportive network that extends beyond the romantic partnership. By solving the problem of attracting and maintaining a healthy relationship, women can experience profound personal and relational fulfillment, leading to a happier, more balanced life.

By letting go of this emotional baggage, you free yourself from the past and open up to new, healthier possibilities. When you know what you want and need in a relationship, you can set boundaries and make decisions that align with your well-being. This clarity fosters mutual respect and understanding, forming a solid foundation for a healthy, fulfilling relationship. Ultimately, this process empowers you to break free from negative patterns and create a love life that is both positive and sustainable.

When we are in a loving, supportive partnership, it significantly enhances our overall well-being, providing emotional stability, companionship, and a sense of purpose. Conversely, being in an unhealthy or unfulfilling relationship can lead to emotional distress, decreased self-esteem, and even physical health issues.

As women, it is essential to learn to articulate our values and needs, set healthy boundaries, and communicate effectively, all crucial skills for maintaining a long-lasting relationship. This transformation not only attracts the right partner, but also fosters a sense of inner confidence and clarity.

Healthy relationships contribute to personal growth, mutual respect, and a harmonious living environment. They serve as a foundation for building families, achieving personal goals, and creating a supportive network that extends beyond the romantic partnership. By solving the problem of attracting and maintaining a healthy relationship, women can experience profound personal and relational fulfillment, leading to a happier, more balanced life.

Dating is harder today than a decade ago.

According to Pew Research Center, nearly half of Americans (47%) believe dating is harder today than a decade ago, with women significantly more likely to hold this view. Key challenges include the increased risk of scams and deception, the impersonal nature of online dating, and shifting societal expectations.

However, there are effective strategies that people are using to overcome these challenges. For instance, positive communication techniques and understanding partner dynamics are crucial. Research by John Gottman, who studied thousands of couples over 30 years, emphasizes the importance of creating a positive interaction environment, where partners support and understand each other deeply, forming the basis of a healthy, lasting relationship.

Additionally, technology has become a double-edged sword in the dating world. While 41% of those who find dating easier today attribute it to technological advancements, many also struggle with the distraction it causes in relationships.

Around 40% of partnered adults report being bothered by their partner's phone use.

Moreover, understanding and addressing behaviors that damage relationships is critical. Many women unintentionally emasculate their partners by withholding appreciation, criticizing, or not trusting them, leading to negative relational outcomes. Recognizing and changing these behaviors can significantly improve relationship satisfaction and longevity.

By integrating these insights and focusing on positive, supportive interaction and effective use of technology, individuals can navigate the complexities of modern dating and build fulfilling, long-lasting relationships.

Dating and relationships: Key findings on views and experiences in the US | Pew Research Center](https://www.pewresearch.org/short-reads/2020/08/20/key-takeaways-on-americans-views-of-and-experiences-with-dating-and-relationships/)

Dating and Relationships | Pew Research Center](https://www.pewresearch.org/internet/2020/05/08/dating-and-relationships-in-the-digital-age

All about Social Proof for new solutions to an old age problem.

These methods are supported by both research and social proof. One of the key resources is "The Queen's Code" by Alison Armstrong, which has helped countless women transform their relationships by understanding and appreciating men. Armstrong's work emphasizes the importance of recognizing and valuing the unique qualities of men, leading to more harmonious and fulfilling relationships.

Studies show that positive communication and mutual respect are critical for relationship success. Couples who engage in positive interactions and constructive conflict resolution, with respect and appreciation are more likely to have long-lasting relationships.

Additionally, there are numerous testimonials and case studies, on Alison Armstrong's website, from women who have applied these principles provide compelling social proof. Women have reported significant improvements in their relationships. They describe experiencing deeper emotional connections, reduced conflict, and increased mutual respect and understanding.

One case study involves a woman who struggled with constant arguments and dissatisfaction in her marriage. After applying the principles from "The Queen's Code," she learned to communicate more effectively and appreciate her husband's efforts, resulting in a marked improvement in their relationship. Similar stories abound, showcasing the transformative power of these methods.

Your 30-Day Challenge

I offer you this 30-Day Challenge so you can also attract and maintain a happy, healthy, and harmonious relationship.

[Dating and Relationships in the Digital Age | Pew Research Center] (https://www.pewresearch.org/internet/2020/05/08/dating-and-relationships-in-the-digital-age/).

Week One: Getting Clear

Identify what you don't and do want in a partner. Reflect

on who you need to be to attract that ideal partner. Write a detailed paragraph about your ideal relationship. Read it every morning and night.

Week Two: No More Criticizing
Stop punishing men. Notice your thoughts about men. Notice women punishing men and see how men react. Notice if you think men need to be punished for misbehaving and what was expected.

Week Three: Using Men's Language

Acknowledge him as a provider. Notice what men are already giving you or taking care of and what it provides for you. Before asking for something, think about what it would provide for you and tell him as part of your request. Once completed, tell him what it provided for you and how much you appreciate his efforts. This will encourage him to do more for you because men get great satisfaction from providing as they think so much of us. This goes for all men.

Week Four: Empowered Communication

Engage in active listening by asking a question and listening attentively without interrupting them. Give him space to express himself fully until complete. Do not ask another question until they have completely answered the first question. This will help you develop healthy communication. By the end of this challenge, you will have transformed your approach to relationships, equipping yourself with the tools to attract and maintain a happy, healthy, and harmonious long-lasting relationship.

Tips for Attracting Your Ideal Partner eBook
https://www.canva.com/design/DAEUu93XHr8/
X6WtzGZ6pYrHbIQ9znV_IA/view?utm_
content=DAEUu93XHr8&utm_campaign=designshare&utm_
medium=link&utm_source=viewer#1

About the Author

As a certified life coach specializing in dating and relationships, Donna Barron's passion is helping women attract their ideal partner and maintain a fun and fulfilling relationship beyond the honeymoon stage. After a 22-year relationship, Donna found herself in a challenging divorce with three small children.

She says, "For ten years, I lived alone with my children, a time marked by frustration and loneliness. Nights were especially difficult, staring at a cold, empty bed, longing for someone to cuddle up with. Seeing happy couples around me only intensified my unhappiness and depression. Even antidepressants and numbing myself with alcohol failed to bring relief. Determined not to spend the rest of my life alone, I embarked on a journey of self-discovery and research. Through this process, I found the solution that led me to the man of my dreams.

Today, I enjoy the best relationship of my life, one that exceeds all my desires. Motivated by my transformation, I decided to help other women struggling to find their soulmate. With my unique perspective on men and what motivates them, I provide women with an advantage in the dating world, guiding them towards the fulfilling and loving relationships they deserve."

Donna Barron
Donna D Barron Coaching
donna@donnadbarroncoaching.com https://www.

facebook.com/donna.barron.9/

"You must never be fearful about what you are doing when it's right."

— Rosa Parks

KIM RILEY

Dedication

To my husband, Roy, for giving me the grace and independence to work on my passion in business, and for his love and presence that helps keep our 35-year marriage alive and thriving!

CHAPTER 15

RENEW AND REVITALIZE: 30 DAYS TO RE-CREATE LOVE & INTIMACY

By Kim Riley

Stepping back from the Brink.

The core problem in the intimate relationship is that it's on the brink of dissolution or divorce. The primary issue addressed in this 30-day challenge is the woman's lack of self-awareness and inability to recognize her role in causing problems in the relationship. She hasn't established strong personal boundaries nor effectively communicated her needs and desires. She feels resentful, blames her partner, and believes he disregards her interests and values. They experienced love and joy when they first met, but now she believes they have fallen out of love.

She needs to become more aware of her needs and boundaries and learn to communicate them so her partner will begin to listen to and respect her. She must acquire skills to communicate effectively and express her love in a way he can receive it, and in a way she can meet his needs alongside her own.

The 30-day challenge will assist her in becoming more self-aware so that she can realize how her negative energy and resentment is making her partner angry and shutting him down. She will become more attuned to her personal presence and energy, and how it affects her and her partner's beliefs and actions. She will master four foundational embodiment practices that will enable her to become more present in the moment so she can get out of her worrying mind, be less triggered by her partner and better able to observe her own beliefs and actions and how they affect her partner and the relationship.

Remembering all the Effort and Investment

Saving the relationship from dissolution matters because women are about to lose a relationship, they and their partners have invested years of time building and creating together. They have developed through their formative adult years together and may have children together who have grown into thriving young adults themselves. They have also supported each other through the years to resolve challenges of their own and challenges they've had in their relationship. To have all of what they share and have built together fall apart is tragic.

Saving the relationship matters because the women will rekindle their love for themselves and their partners and be able to express that love freely. They will feel beautiful inside and out, and will bask in their feminine essence and energy, feeling the confidence and joy they deserve as independent women and as loving partners. And, they will have a great sex life again!

Having these things happen will benefit everything in their lives because they will be able to express their true love for their partners and feel loved in return. They will be giddy with that love-at-first-sight feeling and live in awe and wonder of the dream they are now living, like what it felt like when they and their partners first fell in love years ago. They will feel adored and respected by their partners, and sexy and alive with their newfound confidence and love for themselves and who they are as women.

Are the current intervention methods really saving Marriages?

There are a handful of most popular methods used by professional therapists and counselors in working with couples to solve their relationship problems. Most aim to improve communication and connection between the two partners. (https://www.betterhelp.com/advice/therapy/what-is-the-best-type-of-relationship-therapy/)

John Gottman, one of the most renowned American psychologists in the field of marital stability and founder of the Gottman Institute, developed the Gottman Method, which emphasizes affection, respect, and intimacy as strategies for healthy conflict resolution and managing distress, and highlights the importance of teamwork.

Susan Johnson, another world-renowned therapist, developed a method that many counselors and therapists use for working with couples called Emotionally Focused Therapy (EFT). EFT focuses on emotional sensitivity and vulnerability with the goal of expanding emotional responses between partners, safeguarding the bond they have with each other and creating healthier interactions with each other.

Other common approaches in counseling couples include positive psychology talk therapy that emphasizes communication skills and enables couples to explore and appreciate happy moments as they occur using mindfulness techniques, narrative therapy that involves externalizing conflicts within a relationship through role playing and seeing specific situations from an outside perspective in order to manage conflict effectively, communication analysis that focuses on how couples interact and communicate with each other, and Cognitive Behavioral Therapy and Imago Therapy in which conflict is used as a means to a solution rather than a problem and the therapist offers support by helping the couple develop solutions based on the lessons they learn from their conflicts.

Women's awareness is a game changer.

The solution of women becoming more self-aware as they master their personal presence and energy works toward resolving their relationship problems because they become more confident and sure of themselves and recognize how their energy affects the way they communicate with their partners, listen to them and are listened to by them, and how the nature of their behavior attracts or repels.

Becoming self-aware improves their happiness with themselves, allowing them to be responsible for their thoughts and behaviors and how they impact their partners, and being present in the moment allows them to become more attentive and engaged. They are not distracted and can pay attention to what their partners are saying. This creates an environment of open communication, trust, and understanding, and when they are fully present, they are better equipped to respond in a calm and empathetic manner, which helps to diffuse tense situations with their partners and foster a sense of closeness and intimacy.

The words of one woman represent the sentiments of many struggling in their partnerships: "I had been doing things the same way in life and expecting a different result, the definition of insanity. I used conventional wisdom and psychology to solve emotional and interpersonal problems and had success, yet some of the most painful problems [in my relationship] persisted. I used all the skills I knew and now I have new skills with feminine presence. I think energy work was a huge missing piece to my problem-solving basket of tricks. Now that I have more tools and skills, I feel hopeful."

Women who participate in this challenge will receive one instructional video each week for four weeks in which Kim will demonstrate visually on screen, using her own body energetics, how to engage in four foundational embodiment practices to increase personal presence. The four include Womb Space to ground and stabilize the body, enabling women to get out of their worrying minds; Energetic Presence, which enables women to become aware of how their energy affects those in their presence; Vertical Core, which allows women to connect their hearts with their minds so that they can speak with love and empathy; and Open to Receive, which brings women into an energetic and mental space of receiving love and abundance from others.

Instructional worksheets and blank journal pages will accompany each video for participants to read about each practice and write down their experiences ongoingly of how they feel and interact with their partners.

For 7 consecutive days, the women will engage with the practice of the week and use it every time they are with and/or in conversation with their partners. Each of the four practices will build on the one learned the previous week, so by the end of the 30 days, they will have the basic skills to master their personal presence and enable them to stay calm, grounded and confident when speaking to their partners. The effects of their new energy on their partners' presence and their own feelings of joy and calm will be palpable.

About the Author

Kim Riley is a Relationship Renewal Expert. For as long as she can remember, she has been fascinated by human psychology, personal development, and building strong relationships. The name of her company, Living Connection, exemplifies what she stands for. People are all connected as human beings, yet they often live in separation and divisiveness against each other. Kim is on a mission to help people connect and live with each other in peace and harmony . As a happily married woman of 35 years and counting, her passion is to help couples in long-term partnerships repair the hurt and divisiveness between each other to rekindle their love and create the most passionate and joyful relationship they have ever had.

Kim holds a Master's Degree in Public Health Behavior and Education, as well as life coach certifications in Strategic Intervention based on human needs psychology and transformational life coaching. She is also a certified teacher of the Art of Feminine Presence, providing women with tools to help them develop a physical and energetic presence that attracts the attention and respect they want and deserve in their relationships - most importantly in the one with their life-long partner they committed "until death do us part".

Download the Connect To Your Inner Energy & Joy meditation audio track, guiding you through a 3-step process to tune into your physical, emotional, and energetic well-being. Daily practice of this meditation helps you connect to your overall energy state. By becoming still, observing, and feeling these states without judgment, you can transform your relationship. This practice allows you to tap into your desire for passion and love, positively impacting your connection with your partner.

The call to action is to download a meditation audio track, guiding the client through a 3-step process to tune into her physical, emotional, and energetic well-being. Daily practice of this meditation helps her connect to her overall energy state. By becoming still, observing, and feeling these states without judgment, she can transform her relationship. This practice allows her to tap into her desire for passion and love, positively impacting her connection with her partner. https://go.kimrileycoaching.com/book

Kim Riley
Living Connection LLC
kim@kimrileycoaching.com
https://www.linkedin.com/in/kimriley/

Darlene Williams

Dedication
To my beloved mother, Lucille,

Your unwavering kindness, boundless patience, and sweet spirit made you the perfect example of a mother and grandmother. You transformed our house into a home, filling it with love and warmth that drew in both the young and old. Your legacy of love and gentleness continues to inspire me every day. This chapter is dedicated to you, with all my love and gratitude. Forever in my heart.

CHAPTER 16

DEEPENING YOUR RELATIONSHIP WITH YOUR KIDS AND GRANDKIDS IN 30 DAYS

By Darlene Williams

Slipping through the cracks.

Let's face it, life gets busy, and it's easy to let our relationships with our kids and grandkids slip through the cracks. You might find yourself feeling disconnected, frustrated, or unsure of how to bridge the gap. Maybe you're wondering if your efforts to connect really make a difference, or if you're even on the same wavelength. It's challenging to know how to communicate effectively, stay engaged, and foster meaningful connections across different personalities and generations

Life is hectic, and maintaining strong relationships with our kids and grandkids often becomes challenging. Between work, household responsibilities, and social obligations, it's easy for these bonds to weaken. As a result, feelings of disconnection and frustration can arise, leaving you unsure of how to bridge the gap.

One of the main difficulties lies in communication. Different generations often have varying communication styles, preferences, and interests, making it hard to stay on the same wavelength. You might find yourself questioning whether your efforts to connect are truly impactful or if they are perceived as intrusive or out of touch.

Staying engaged is another significant challenge. With the fast pace of modern life and the pervasive influence of technology, finding common ground can feel daunting. Kids and grandkids might be absorbed in their digital worlds, while you might prefer more traditional forms of interaction. This disparity can create a sense of alienation and uncertainty about how to foster meaningful connections.

Additionally, each individual's unique personality adds another layer of complexity. Tailoring your approach to suit different temperaments and preferences requires patience and adaptability, which can be exhausting amidst other life demands.

Ultimately, the goal is to build and maintain relationships that are nurturing and fulfilling for both you and your loved ones. However, achieving this involves overcoming the barriers of communication gaps, generational differences, and individual personalities, all while juggling the myriad of responsibilities that come with everyday life.

Knowing the most important and rewarding parts of life.

Solving this problem matters because your relationship with your kids and grandkids is one of the most important and rewarding parts of life. When these relationships are strong, it brings joy, support, and a sense of fulfillment that nothing else can match. Imagine the satisfaction of knowing you're a positive influence in their lives, helping them grow and succeed. When you communicate effectively, you're not just talking—you're connecting, understanding, and truly being there for each other.

Think about the confidence and happiness that comes from knowing your efforts are appreciated and making a real difference. When your family feels your genuine support and interest, it builds a foundation of trust and love that withstands life's challenges. You become their rock, the one they can turn to for advice, comfort, and shared moments of joy.

Creating this connection also ensures that family traditions and values are passed down, giving your kids and grandkids a strong sense of identity and belonging. It's about more than just getting along—it's about creating memories, fostering growth, and building a legacy that will be remembered for generations.

By addressing this issue, you're not only improving your own life but also positively impacting the lives of those you care about most. You'll see stronger bonds, better communication, and a happier, more united family. This transformation leads to a more fulfilling and meaningful life, where every moment shared is a cherished part of your family's story. Let's make those connections deeper and more meaningful together.

All about intentional action. Setting a Blueprint for positive results.

To deepen my own relationship with my kids and grandkids, I created a blueprint to help me communicate better, spend quality time together, and create a positive, supportive environment. I learned how to truly listen and respond to my loved ones in ways that resonate with them and make them feel appreciated by me. Within a month, I began to see a noticeable shift in my relationship with each of them. I now feel more connected, valued, and understood by them too because they feel your genuine effort and interest in their lives. I know I am now building a lasting legacy of love and connection for all of my family.

Other grandparents, who tried these methods, report feeling closer, more understood, and more appreciated. They all saw their children and grandchildren light up when they engaged in activities they love or when they took the time to really listen to understand their perspectives. They also found that these approaches make everyday interactions more enjoyable and fulfilling.

These changes don't happen overnight, with consistent effort, the transformation is undeniable.

Whether it's finding new ways to communicate, discovering shared interests, or creating a positive home environment, each strategy is designed to resonate with different personalities and needs.

This 30-Day Guide is designed to transform your relationships by providing practical, actionable steps tailored to your unique family dynamics so you can also create a lasting legacy of love and connection. .

Week 1: Open Communication
◆ **Day 1-2:** Have sit-down conversations with each family member. Listen actively.
◆ **Day 3-4:** Share a meaningful story from your past. Encourage them to share one too.
◆ **Day 5-7:** Schedule daily check-ins to ask about their day and share yours.

Week 2: Quality Time
- ◆ **Day 8-10:** Engage in activities they enjoy, like games or cooking.
- ◆ **Day 11-13:** Establish a family tradition, such as weekly movie night or Sunday brunch.
- ◆ **Day 14:** Reflect on the week's activities and plan to repeat favorites.

Week 3: Positive Environment
- ◆ **Day 15-16:** Write notes of appreciation for each family member.
- ◆ **Day 17-19:** Create a positive home environment by decluttering together or setting up a cozy family area.
- ◆ **Day 20-21:** Celebrate small successes from the past week, like good grades or completed projects.

Week 4: Shared Stories and Skills
- ◆ **Day 22-24:** Share another personal story or tradition. Teach a hobby.
- ◆ **Day 25-27:** Learn something new from them, like a tech trick or a favorite hobby.
- ◆ **Day 28:** Plan a family day with activities contributed by everyone.

Final Days: Reflection and Adaptation
- ◆ **Day 29:** Hold a family meeting to reflect on the month.
- ◆ **Day 30:** Plan to continue these practices with regular check-ins and new activities.

"The Ultimate Guide to Spoiling Your Kids and Grandkids" Complimentary Discovery Call and Companion Cheat Sheet. Moms and grandmas, envision a future free of financial stress, filled with unforgettable moments and a secure legacy for your loved ones. During your No-Charge Discovery Call, I will support you in elevating your relationships with your children and grandchildren. Click the link and start transforming your family's future today!

https://storage.googleapis.com/msgsndr/
yesRb14A2CxyudJOUrJr/media/665a98d9c6bcc8e4d2dc01e3.
pdf

About the Author

Hi! I'm Darlene Williams, a passionate mom and grandma dedicated to helping you elevate your relationships with your kids and grandkids. As a mom and grandma myself, I know how important it is to spoil the kids without breaking the bank. I support other moms and grandmas who want to give their children and grandchildren the attention they deserve, even when funds are tight.

I discovered how to create strong, lasting bonds with your family. Together, we'll build meaningful connections and a legacy of wealth that will benefit generations to come. Imagine giving your loved ones the best of both worlds: the love and attention they crave, and the financial security to pursue their dreams.

I believe in truly listening to our children and grandchildren so they feel heard and valued. Spending quality time and being present with them is my top priority. Let's focus on what matters most and create joyous, fulfilling relationships. Join me on this journey to elevate your family's connections and leave a lasting legacy of love and prosperity.

Darlene Williams
Legacy Wealth Expert
darlene@darlenewilliams.com
https://www.linkedin.com/in/darlene-williams-helping-coaches-attract-more-clients-faster-82017137/

Conclusion

Reaching your first milestone is vital because it boosts motivation, validates your efforts, builds confidence, provides clear direction, offers emotional benefits, and helps in tracking progress. This early success sets a positive tone for the entire journey, making it more likely that you will achieve your ultimate goal.

For the second half of our compilation, we focus on Becoming Your Best-Self, the link between Wellness and our best life, and finally how all of it impacts our relationships.

Susan Patterson's: *Claim Your Confidence*. In this chapter, I will focus on increased abundance, problem-solving through creative innovation, and pursuing more opportunities. When a woman claims her confidence, i.e., her power, she experiences a profound transformation. Becoming more confident has multiple positive results - ranging from improved health to happiness and mental well-being to greater satisfaction in relationships. This is clear to anyone who meets her; she can command respect where it did not previously exist and command attention in situations where she was previously overlooked or ignored.

Stacey Hall Guides us on *How to Harness Your Power and Achieve Your Goals.* Did you know that all matter and energy are in constant motion and vibration? This is known as "The Universal Law of Vibration." It highlights the importance of aligning our internal frequencies with the reality we wish to manifest. By aligning our inner world with these frequencies, we unlock infinite possibilities and potential for growth, expansion, and fulfillment of our goals. Even more remarkable is that we can access these possibilities in as little as 30 days!

Loralee Humpherys challenges us to *Elevate Your Life: 30 Days to Pain-Free Digestion.* Do you wish you were more productive – like you once were? If it wasn't for the exhaustion, brain fog and stress ball sitting in your gut? This is an indication that your digestion is off. When it's not working properly, neither are you! Compromised gut health adversely affects every area of life. Why live with pain, discomfort and inflammation? Popping aspirins, antacids and laxatives, thinking they'll make it away? The root cause of gut issues is known. With the proven techniques to rebuild your digestion shared in this chapter; you can heal yourself and gain control of your health.

Cheri Petroni shows us how to *Harmonize Your Body's Energies to Boost Wealth.* Let's face it, we all have moments when we simply feel "off". That feeling is a symptom of an energy imbalance. The body's energy is comprised of physical, emotional, mental, and spiritual energy centers. When they aren't working in unison, our bodies experience misalignment. Think of these energy centers as parts of a car. When a car gets a tune-up it runs smoothly. Similarly, aligned energy centers are "tuned up" to bring awareness, fuel passion, and drive action. A body in balance leads to greater success opportunities.

Monika Greczek reminds us that Executive Presence and Confidence begins with *Gorgeous and Healthy Hair in 30 Days!* It is essential to overall well-being to adopt a holistic approach to achieving optimal scalp health. In this chapter, "I will provide a 30-Day hair and scalp plan for detoxification, using scalp care and sulphate-free clarifying shampoos to remove impurities and product buildup. Then to nourishment through deep conditioning treatments, exfoliating scrubs, and hydrating oils. Followed by infusions of protein, with ingredients like egg and yogurt to strengthen hair follicles and reduce breakage. And finally, on maintenance and protection, with essential oil massages, leave-in conditioners, and daily tips on hydration and balanced nutrition to support long-term scalp health and hair growth."

Donna Barron's powerful message to *Becoming Irresistible: How to Attract Your Ideal Partner* The proven tips in this chapter are designed to help you become the woman that a man truly wants and desires. You will learn and practice healthy communication skills, empowering you to express yourself authentically and understand your partner better. You will feel empowered, gaining a profound understanding of men and what motivates them in relationships to equip you with the confidence and clarity to move forward in your love life. By the end of the 30 days, you will have the tools and mindset needed to attract and build a lasting, fulfilling relationship that brings you happiness and harmony.

Kim Riley brings it home with *Renew and Revitalize: 30 Days to Re-Create Love & Intimacy*. This 30-day challenge is for midlife women feeling frustrated and distant in their long-term relationships who want to save them from dissolution. It focuses on self-awareness and personal presence to resolve relationship issues through weekly embodiment practices:

Womb Space - Grounding the body.
Energetic Presence - Understanding personal energy.
Vertical Core - Connecting heart and mind.
Open to Receive - Welcoming love and abundance.

Led by Relationship Renewal Expert Kim, participants will develop skills to enhance communication and rekindle intimacy. The challenge includes a meditation audio track to tune into physical, emotional, and energetic well-being, fostering love and passion in their relationships with their partners.

Darlene Williams closes our compilation by reminding of what truly matters in our lives our Legacy, our Bloodline. ***Deepening Your Relationship with Your Kids and Grandkids in 30 Days*** This chapter is about elevating your relationships with your kids and grandkids by improving communication, spending quality time together, and creating a positive home environment. Through a 30-day challenge with practical steps, you'll foster deeper connections, better understand each other, and build a stronger family bond. With my guidance, you'll see your efforts transform into more meaningful, joyful interactions and a lasting legacy of love and support. Let's embark on this journey together to enrich your family life and create unforgettable memories.

We hope this book has the desired effect the author's hearts and thought leadership had in mind. Their calls to action and gifts are meant as a

1. Motivation Boost

<u>Sense of Achievement:</u> Achieving a milestone provides a tangible sense of accomplishment, which boosts motivation and encourages you to keep going.

Momentum: It creates positive momentum, making it easier to tackle subsequent steps and maintain progress towards your ultimate goal.

2. Validation of Efforts

Proof of Progress: It validates that your efforts and strategies are working, reinforcing the belief that your goal is attainable.

Encouragement: Seeing concrete progress can dispel doubts and fears, encouraging you to stay committed to the process.

3. Building Confidence

Self-Efficacy: Successfully reaching a milestone enhances your confidence in your abilities, increasing your self-efficacy and the likelihood of continued success.

Overcoming Initial Hurdles: Initial milestones often involve overcoming significant obstacles, proving to yourself that you can handle challenges.

4. Clear Path Forward

Direction and Focus: Milestones help break down a larger goal into manageable steps, providing clear direction and focus. Each milestone reached clarifies the path ahead.

Adjustments: Reaching a milestone allows you to assess your progress and make any necessary adjustments to your plan or approach.

5. Emotional and Psychological Benefits

<u>Positive Reinforcement:</u> Achieving milestones provides positive reinforcement, releasing feel-good chemicals in the brain like dopamine, which can enhance mood and drive.

<u>Reduced Anxiety:</u> Breaking a goal into milestones can reduce anxiety and overwhelm by making the goal seem more manageable and less daunting.

6. Accountability and Tracking

<u>Progress Tracking:</u> Milestones serve as checkpoints that help you track your progress and stay accountable. They provide measurable benchmarks to evaluate your success.

<u>Milestones as Feedback:</u> They act as feedback mechanisms, allowing you to celebrate small wins and understand what works, which can be critical for maintaining long-term focus.

May you reach your 30 Days Challenge and begin your journey of Transformation.

This compilation was
Curated by: Stacey Hall
Design and layout by: Dortha Hise
Cover by: Kristina Conatser
Published by: Dr. Carolina M. Billings,
Founder and CEO PWT Multi-Media Publishing.

"Women belong in all places where decisions are being made. It shouldn't be that women are the exception."

— Ruth Bader Ginsburg

About Powerful women today & pwt publishing

POWERFUL WOMEN TODAY IS A GLOBAL COMMUNITY of Highly Influential Women Entrepreneurs and Professional Women Who Want to Make a Difference in The World by Showcasing Their Voice, Expertise, Talents, Experience and Passion

Empowerment is about taking action... No more apologies to anyone by any woman ever again when you embrace empowerment! Especially no apologies for being true to yourself and for going after what you want. Powerful Women are fierce defenders of joy, happiness and independence and honour themselves and their own decisions.

As women, we are often taught in society to be good girls, get good grades, get a job, get married, and have children. But luckily times have changed for women today — we now have the choice to be powerful and live life by our own set of rules. Powerful Women's greatest gifts are to trust their intuition and to learn to put themselves first so they can be the best unique version of themselves, and give back to the world — Unapologetically!

MISSION

To Champion and Empower Women's Emotional and Financial Independence.

VISION

To Champion Emotionally Independent women with literacy and maturity who have agency, and know how to negotiate win/win/win solutions that serve not only the world but self. She knows to have intelligent, productive and timely conversations that lead to desired outcomes. She knows that it is self-accountability not blaming others that leads to success.

A Financial Independent woman does not have to compromise her values, self-worth, and builds the life she deserves for herself and those she leads and serves. A woman with Financial Literacy has Emotional Maturity that leads to Freedom.

OUR CORE VALUES

We believe,
In Courage
In Character
In Supporting and Championing

In Resolution and Reconciliation

In Responsibility
In Action not Words

In Honouring Diversity and Active Inclusion

In Free Will and Self Agency

We believe,
That there is an opportunity for Greatness at Powerful
Women Today

That We are #StrongerTogether
That Empowered Women must Empower Women
That There are no problems but opportunities for growth

That Our Differences are our Blessings that must be
Honoured Respect above all else.
That Deeds Speak, Intentions Whisper
In Giving before Receiving.

OUR ECOSYSTEM

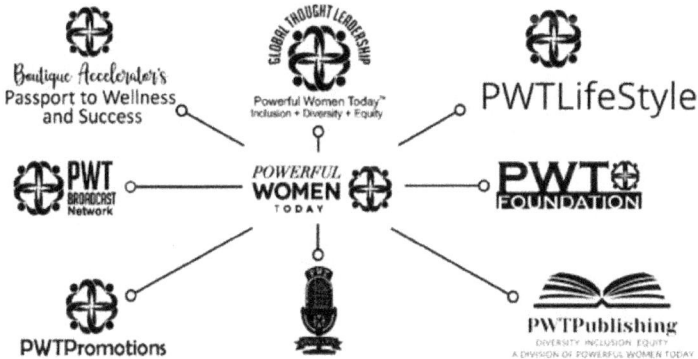

Visit our Website:
www.powerfulwomentoday.com

Contact us at:
Publisher@powerfulwomentoday.com

Join our Newsletter:
https://www.linkedin.com/
newsletters/6861823529403465728/

Follow us on Social Media:
www.linkedin.com/in/carolinabillings/
www.youtube.com/channel/
UCkl5hW2Z5Uz3daMxQFVRE_w

Join our Global Network:
https://powerful-women-today.mn.co/share/tu-
t4J8RU7G87qj7?utm_source=manual

Check the latest issue of our Magazine:
https://www.pwtmagazine.com/

PWTPublishing

DIVERSITY INCLUSION EQUITY

A DIVISION OF POWERFUL WOMEN TODAY

WHAT IF YOU HAD EVERYTHING YOU NEED TO PUBLISH A BESTSELLING BOOK ALL IN ONE PLACE?

Most people I meet all around the world have an ingrained belief that writing a book is an insurmountable task that is only for those with a literary degree, not a coach, consultant, practitioner, speaker, healer or entrepreneur... and up until recently, it was!

DITCH YOUR FEARS, NOT YOUR DREAMS
WRITE YOUR BOOK NOW

We believe it is the time in history for women to begin to document their journey and stories. **Throughout history, women have played a major role** in scientific discovery, literature and the arts **yet their names have been omitted or forgotten.**

PWTPublishing a division of Powerful Women Today is committed to **Diversity, Equity and Inclusion of all voices ready to share their gifts and thought leadership with the world.** We specialize primarily in removing barriers to entry for women authors and those who **champion women's advancement**, safety and progress. **Our multi-media publishing style maximizes the author's visibility**

and content distribution. Are you ready to make history? Our point of difference is that we provide a package that includes all the mentoring, content structure, editing, layout, publishing, Amazon Bestseller Campaign, upload and eBook, pre-launch, and marketing guidance. We also give group support in private, author-only groups.

TOP 5 REASONS TO PUBLISH

1. To Build a Brand & Grow Your Business
2. To Build a Legacy
3. For Thought Leadership
4. To Fundraise
5. Publishing as Income

www.powerfulwomentoday.com

www.ingramcontent.com/pod-product-compliance
Lightning Source LLC
Chambersburg PA
CBHW040856210326
41597CB00029B/4865